PRAISE FOR
AWFUL BEAUTIFUL
LIFE

"The sad irony of the title of Becky Powell's book, AWFUL BEAUTIFUL LIFE, is not lost on those of us who know her and her children. Becky's bravery in the face of tragedy is an inspiration to us all."

—Tim McClure, author, *Don't Mess with Texas*

"When faced with devastating loss and deception, Becky showed the world, through her faith, how to handle heartbreak with humility and sincere grace."

—Julie and Ben Crenshaw

"Becky Powell is a strong lady who has integrity, honesty, and unequivocal faith. Becky is a dedicated mother who teaches her children these values. When Becky faced a dark chapter in her life, it took all of these qualities to see her through to the light at the end of the tunnel. We are all grateful to have Becky in our lives. She is a role model that we should all strive to become. Becky: Well done, our friend!"   —Linda and Michael McCaul

"Uncommon courage in the face of great adversity—that captures the actions of Becky Powell in untangling affairs and ensuring damage to others was contained. This is an inspiring story."

—Bobby R. Inman, Admiral, U.S. Navy (Retired)

Faith, funny, spread to! Blessings, Becky

awful beautiful life

When God Shows Up
in the Midst of Tragedy

BECKY POWELL
AND KATHERINE REAY

Faith
Words

New York   Nashville

FaithWords
Hachette Book Group
1290 Avenue of the Americas, New York, NY 10104
faithwords.com
twitter.com/faithwords

First Edition: December 2019

FaithWords is a division of Hachette Book Group, Inc. The FaithWords name and
logo are trademarks of Hachette Book Group, Inc.

The publisher is not responsible for websites (or their content) that are not owned
by the publisher.

The Hachette Speakers Bureau provides a wide range of authors for speaking
events. To find out more, go to www.hachettespeakersbureau.com or call (866)
376-6591.

All Scripture quotations, unless otherwise indicated, are taken from the Holy Bible,
New International Version®, NIV®. Copyright ©1973, 1978, 1984, 2011 by
Biblica, Inc.™ Used by permission of Zondervan. All rights reserved worldwide.
www.zondervan.com The "NIV" and "New International Version" are trademarks
registered in the United States Patent and Trademark Office by Biblica, Inc.™

Library of Congress Cataloging-in-Publication Data
Names: Powell, Rebecca, author.
Title: Awful beautiful life : when God shows up in the midst of tragedy /
Rebecca Powell and Katherine Reay.
Description: first [edition]. | New York : Faith Words, 2019.
Identifiers: LCCN 2019011726 | ISBN 9781546035558 (hardcover) | ISBN
9781549150111 (audio download) | ISBN 9781546035572 (ebook)
Subjects: LCSH: Widows--Religious life. | Suicide--Religious
aspects--Christianity. | Bereavement--Religious aspects--Christianity. |
Grief--Religious aspects--Christianity. | Consolation.
Classification: LCC BV4908 .P69 2019 | DDC 248.8/66082--dc23
LC record available at https://lccn.loc.gov/2019011726

ISBNs: 978-1-5460-3555-8 (hardcover), 978-1-5460-3557-2 (ebook)

Printed in the United States of America

LSC-C

10 9 8 7 6 5 4 3 2

To Madison, Boone, and John Luke:
I am so proud of all of you.
Always love each other
and <u>pursue</u> God.
✖❤🙂👰⛪

For Mary.
All my love,
Katherine

You can't really smile until you've shed some tears...

—"Awful Beautiful Life" by Darryl Worley

AUTHOR'S NOTE

Within these pages, you'll find the story of my family's journey after my husband, Mark, committed suicide on May 16, 2013. It's a story of life, tragedy, and the wellspring of love that lifted us. In many ways, it is a call to all of us to love well.

You'll read about how God showed up in our darkest time and carried us through. You'll read about the people involved and the incredible grace and patience they bestowed upon me while I worked to pay back every cent my husband had borrowed. You'll find tears, laughter, faith, and lots of country music within these pages as well.

The heartbreak and hope within country music sustained me through many stormy nights and turned tears to laughter most days. I will forever be thankful to Gary Allan and his song "Every Storm (Runs Out of Rain)." I trusted in that truth as firmly as I trusted Psalm 34:8: "Taste and see that the Lord is good; blessed is the one who takes refuge in him."

Sometimes—oftentimes—we feel both truths only after the storm is behind us, but that doesn't mean that bright horizon wasn't always there.

—*Becky Powell*
December 2019

Chapter 1

Don't go looking for the reasons.
Don't go asking Jesus why.

—"Broken Halos" by Chris Stapleton

In all good stories, you have to understand who the character was to enjoy the journey to who she becomes. It's no different here, I guess, for fiction often tells the truth about life, and life is often stranger than fiction. My story begins as a perfect fairy tale.

If you knew my family around Christmas 2012, you were probably invited to our annual Christmas party. On the first Wednesday of every December, my husband, Mark, and I, along with our friends the Dalgleishes, hosted a Christmas party for 450 guests at our home. The party was so big—both in its size and grandeur—that the *Austin American Statesman* featured our 2011 festivities as *the* event where Democrats and

Republicans raised a glass together. "Everyone" in town knew—even if your invitation got lost in the mail—to show up at our house at six p.m. on that first Wednesday in December, and to bring an unwrapped gift.

We lived in Austin's Tarrytown neighborhood in a sprawling eight-thousand-square-foot home, with a stone exterior and vaulted roof, which gave it a church-like aesthetic that set a perfect backdrop for a Christmas party. The side facing our quiet cul-de-sac was full of windows. During the day, those windows let in gorgeous east-facing light. On that first Wednesday, they high-lighted the bustling party within.

After pulling up to our home, each visitor would hand their keys to a valet, who would take the car and welcome them to the party. On their way up the stone walk, and noting a few friends through the windows, they would drop their unwrapped toy into the sleigh in our front yard. The gifts were for the Rainbow Room at Travis County's Child Protective Services. Each year we collected hundreds of toys for needy kids. Once the gift was nestled among the others, the guest walked up the large stone steps to the front door, where I hugged them. I always stationed myself at the front door since it was the only way to see everyone at least once. I'd tell each guest about their friends who were already inside and wish them a merry Christmas.

Stephen Shallcross's 2 Dine 4 catered the party. Waiters silently passed through the rooms, offering appetizers to the crowd, offering mini beef Wellingtons or the party's signature cocktail, the Powell Mistletoe Martini. They refilled their platters in the carport outside. There were waiters who worked the party every year and remembered the names of the guests, whispering to them that the favorite rosemary almonds were in a silver bowl in the living room this year.

The thirteen-foot Christmas tree sat regally in the living room, and off to the right the dining room table was piled high with Christmas desserts. Scott Calvert at The Cake Plate outdid himself that year. Our twelve-person table overflowed with every sugary delight imaginable: mini gingerbread houses, Christmas tree brownies, glittery bonbons, cake pops, and French macarons. If one walked deeper into our home, saying hello to friends and acquaintances, and enjoying the Christmas music, they'd see the seven fully decorated live trees throughout the house. Martha Stewart had nothing on me that first Wednesday of every December—this party was a labor of love, and the highlight of my year. It ushered in a beautiful, magical, and holy month for me.

Christmas 2012 was particularly memorable because, after celebrating at home, we headed to the Waldorf-Astoria in New York City. Madison, our eldest, was twenty that winter and celebrated her debut at the International Debutante Ball on December 29. It was an extraordinary affair covering four whirlwind days and culminating in a glorious ball with girls in white gowns, each escorted by a young tuxedo-clad man.

We arrived back in Austin just in time for the kids to

return to school and for Mark and me to regroup for a few days before our next trip.

Mark and I always celebrated our December anniversary—twenty-two years in 2012—with a trip in January. It was a special way for us to unwind and reconnect after our busy falls. In January 2013 we headed to Bora Bora for nine days, a land of paradise. We relaxed, lay on the beach, went deep-sea fishing, snorkeled, read books, and thoroughly enjoyed each other's company.

Once our plane touched down in Austin a week later, the new year began in earnest. I went back to my world of work and Mark returned to his...

At that time, I was a stay-at-home mom, living a fairy-tale life. I had groups of close friends, lunched out often, and volunteered across town. Not long ago, a friend told me he felt that during those years I lived for my kids, and my husband made all the decisions. I can't say he was entirely wrong. The bills I paid came from an account Mark funded each month. The plans I made were structured in concert with Mark's work and travel schedules. I volunteered for the Women's Symphony League, Hospice, Young Life, and the Helping Hand Home; I served on the board of the Austin Bridge Builders Alliance, the parents' council at our kids' school, and the guidance committee for Westlake High School. I handled our family schedule and our kids' activities. I orchestrated the tenor of our home. Mark managed the business of it.

Mark worked as managing director of Atlantic Trust

Private Wealth Management in the Austin office. And while his work rarely took him from home, golf trips did. Mark's great passion, besides his family, was golf. He belonged to numerous clubs around the country and was a founding member of Ben Crenshaw's Austin Golf Club and Sand Hills. He played almost every weekend with either friends or our sons, Boone and John Luke. After all, in Austin, one can play golf year-round.

Our next full family trip was spring break in March. We headed to our usual destination, the Ritz-Carlton Hotel in the Cayman Islands.

Our final trip that spring was spent with friends in Turks and Caicos. Along with three other couples, we traveled to the Grace Bay Club to celebrate our dear friend Lisa Stedman's fiftieth birthday in style. We returned to Austin on May 7, 2013.

From the outside, it was a glamorous life. We looked like *that* family. We were *that* family. In photographs, we smiled and looked gloriously happy. And for the most part we were. We took wonderful vacations; Mark and I attended all the named galas; we hosted fund-raising dinners and events for the governor, judges, congressmen, and other statewide politicians; and we volunteered and participated in many of the political, cultural, and philanthropic highlights in town. While one couldn't call us "Old Austin," as neither Mark nor I were born in Austin, we were certainly a staple within its political and cultural life.

Madison, our only daughter, was a sophomore at Baylor

University that spring. She was a communications and public relations major. Our second child, Boone, was eighteen and was approaching high school graduation. We were thrilled he would join Madison at Baylor that fall. John Luke, our youngest, was twelve years old and finishing sixth grade. He too lived for the game of golf and enjoyed regular private lessons with Bill Moretti, one of *Golf* magazine's "Top 100 Instructors." Even at that young age, John Luke had a handicap that turned most men green with envy.

The kids were busy. Mark and I were busy. And the daily routines of our home felt safe and comfortable, warm and welcoming. Mark met with a men's Bible study during the week, and I met with a women's group. While Mark joined friends on the golf course each weekend, my friends dropped by the house most afternoons. We went to church together as a family every Sunday. And for ten years, from 2000 to 2010, we housed Young Life students from the University of Texas in our guest room and held the campus's Young Life bi-monthly meetings in our living room. Our home and our lives were full, varied, and very blessed.

I confess that in looking back, it feels as if our lives ramped up from 2011 to 2013, and by that spring we were truly overscheduled. The tenor of our home had changed without my really noticing it. No longer tied to carpools, since two of my three children drove, Mark and I traveled more, went out more, hosted more political fund-raisers—we simply did *more*. Yet Mark still managed to spend time golfing with our sons and made a special effort for daddy-daughter date nights with Madison. I still cooked every evening we were home and left home-cooked meals for the kids when Mark and I dined out. But rarely did we sit down for a family dinner together as we had only a couple years before. In fact, if we were home, there were usually more people at our table.

I'm an extrovert and love nothing more than having friends and family around. Our home was a gathering place for our kids and their friends, and a gathering place for my friends as well. Friends often dropped by for a glass of wine on their way home and sat to talk while I made dinner. Many would even stay for dinner, perched at our kitchen island, chatting with my kids and their friends as easily as they would with their own children. The kids laughed, saying that our house had a revolving door, and they were more surprised when friends didn't fill our home than when they did.

But that revolving door spun faster the spring of 2013. I was drinking more, a couple glasses of wine each night, and I slept less, often waking in the middle of the night, unable to find sleep again for hours. And just days before we boarded our flight to Turks and Caicos, Mark and I had one of our biggest fights in years. Although the subject matter was a serious and recurring theme in our marriage, Mark's dismissive attitude that morning shocked and infuriated me. He actually said, "It's no big deal" to me and brushed my feelings aside. If someone had taken a picture of me that day—and for a few days after—I would not have looked "gloriously happy."

Upon returning from Turks and Caicos on May 7, life didn't slow, though the school year wound down. On May 18 Boone was heading to his senior prom; Madison, just home from Baylor, was scheduled to leave for a semester in Italy on May 19; John Luke was finishing the school year on May 25; then we were going to celebrate Boone's high school graduation on May 31. With all the year-end projects and celebrations, I still had final details to pull together for Madison's semester abroad.

And there were more trips to plan. We often traveled to Colorado Springs in the summer to see Mark's parents, and we talked about visiting Madison in Italy. But every time I tried to secure dates and book flights, Mark pushed back.

On May 15 Mark made plans for a special family dinner—just the five of us. We'd had a full family dinner at home on the fourteenth, but that night he wanted to go out. He'd planned every detail, saying this was our last night together for many weeks. His golf trip, starting two days later, meant he would miss Madison's departure for Italy. We ate at Uchiko, one of our favorite restaurants, and swapped stories the entire evening. Mark asked the kids loads of fun family questions, including their favorite pet, family memory, and vacation.

Home again, Mark wanted to watch *Caddyshack* with the kids, but I put my foot down. I was all for family fun, but John Luke was too young for the movie's humor. I headed to bed, the kids headed off to their rooms, and Mark sat in the family room strumming his guitar. I drifted to sleep as Mark played the guitar and sang one of his favorite Eagles songs. I felt incredibly blessed. I loved the daily rhythms of our lives and couldn't see that underlying fabric ever changing.

This was who and what we were.

Chapter 2

When I bow my head tonight there'll be no me,
myself, and I . . .

—"All I Ask for Anymore" by Trace Adkins

May 16, 2013, started early for me. May rivals December for busyness, but it never gets the respect. We all expect December to roll us, but the end of school can push just as hard. On that Thursday, I was a couple steps behind before my feet hit the floor. As I rolled out of bed, I glanced back at Mark, still sleeping, and smiled. His request for a special family dinner the night before had been inspired. Yes, it was our last night as a family for several weeks, but it was also a night of more family connection and fun than we'd had in a while.

I leaned over and kissed his cheek. That woke him and, after a longer, deeper kiss, he headed to the shower. I dressed, loaded the car with all I needed for the day, and took our youngest, twelve-year-old John Luke, to school.

After dropping off John Luke, I drove across Austin to volunteer at Helping Hand Home, a residential home for children taken from abusive homes. It's such a special place and only one of seven in Texas equipped to handle such tender children. The committee I was on served lunch to the staff each month. After serving them at noon, my close friend Leslie joined me for a lunch of our own at Asti in Austin's Hyde Park neighborhood. Our friend Dinah, who usually joined us for both the work and the lunch, had left for Russia the day before.

School wasn't even out and summer plans were in full swing. Dinah was already in London on her layover to Russia, Leslie was organizing the last details for her summer in Telluride, and there were a million details to settle for both the boys' summers and for Madison's trip. After lunch, I spent the afternoon running errands.

I arrived home around five o'clock just in time to start dinner. The house was strangely empty. A text soon told me Madison had left moments before with Boone and their older cousin Joey, who lived with us that spring, to catch *Gatsby*, showing at the Barton Creek Mall. John Luke was also out: he had a weekly standing golf game with Jackson, a family friend and Young Life program leader at the University of Texas.

I was standing at the refrigerator when the phone rang.

"I've done something really bad. I love you and the kids and I've left a folder for you in your closet, on the top shelf. You need to follow the instructions exactly."

Mark's voice was tense, but level, directed, and in control.

"Wha—"

He cut me off. "Tell the kids I love them and I love you."

"Mark, wait!" My voice pitched up. "What are you saying? What did you do?" I tripped over my words and questions as dread filled me. "Wait— What— It doesn't matter. Whatever it is, it doesn't matter."

Mark's tone told me there was no quarter. It was a tone he used when decisions were made, and were final. But I found something else in his tone, too—an eerie calm that terrified me. I kept speaking to keep him with me, on the phone, and to get to the bottom of whatever *this* was.

I glanced out the windows to see someone approaching our house.

"Mark?" I spoke into the phone, but watched the woman. She stopped and we stared at each other. "Mark? What is Monte James's wife doing here?"

I caught my words. The woman outside was a friend. Her name was Katherine. But at that moment, something within Mark's voice alerted me that my friend was not approaching our front door. Instead, Mark's lawyer's wife was approaching our front door.

He replied in a level tone, "I love all of you."

I strode the short distance to the door, opened it, and thrust my hand into Katherine's face, palm out with fingers spread wide. "I cannot do this right now."

The phone was in my other hand, pressed to my ear. Mark was silent. There was a quality to the silence that pricked me as I stepped back and slammed the door shut.

Katherine is five-foot-four, petite, and gentle. If I'm not one to shove my hand in someone's face or slam a door, she is certainly not one to stick her foot into it to stop it. Yet that's what she did. The door bounced back into my hand. Eye to eye, she whispered, "I'll be right out here," and turned away.

I called into the phone. "Mark? Mar—"

It was silent. Mark had hung up.

Looking back, it's hard to pinpoint exactly what was going through my mind. Thoughts and questions spun too fast. I grabbed my keys and got into my car, calling Mark. One touch, four rings, then voice mail—again and again. He never answered.

I drove down the street determined to find him, only to turn back at the first corner when I realized I had no idea where to begin my search. I drove the block home and noted Katherine sitting in her car waiting outside my front door.

More questions raced through my mind. *Why is she here? Is she to keep me here? Did her husband send her because Mark has done something wrong?* I didn't have answers, but I needed help. Help I could trust. I placed two short calls as soon as I reached the house.

The first was to my sister, Mary Beth, who lived three

hours away in Houston. "Something's wrong. Please get here now."

My second call was to Jeff Stedman, Mark's best friend. He and his wife, Lisa, lived in Colorado Springs, Colorado. If anyone knew anything, Jeff would. Jeff was about to begin the opening evening for a charity he'd brought to his community, The First Tee, so his phone went to voice mail. Lisa answered her phone and, hearing my voice, promised me Jeff would call me right away.

Seconds later, Jeff called. "I got a package from him today. I'll go get it."

We hung up, and I made another call, this time to Bill Jones, another lawyer and a good friend.

This call was longer because, as former general counsel to Governor Rick Perry, Bill could help me—and Mark—immediately.

Bill heard the panic in my voice, learned Katherine was outside my house, and headed to my house right away. While driving, he called Monte James, Katherine's husband, and learned he had sent her to my house.

He sent her because he knew I would need a friend. Mark had called Monte before calling me, and Monte suspected what lay ahead of us. Mark had emailed him a copy of his employer Atlantic Trust's insurance policy, highlighting its indemnity clause, and had ended their talk with "Take care of Becky and the kids."

Monte too had tried to keep Mark on the phone. When Mark hung up, Monte sent Katherine to me.

In Houston, my sister Mary Beth got into her car immediately.

In Colorado Springs, Jeff opened the package and left his charity event for the Denver airport and the first flight he could catch to Austin.

In Austin, between Bill, Monte, the state troopers, and the local police, everything was being done to find Mark.

I glanced out the windows again and found Katherine had been joined on the front lawn by one of my dearest friends, whom I call my "Austin mom"—with my mom's permission, of course. Kathy Smith's presence made Katherine safe for me, and I let them both in the house. The three of us started to make calls.

It wasn't unlike the scene in *It's a Wonderful Life* when Mary Bailey and Uncle Billy run around town with no more knowledge than I had, but were filled with the certainty that "George is in trouble." Mark was, without a doubt, in serious trouble.

I called Jill Adams. "I can't find Mark and I'm worried something is wrong. You and Mark [her husband] need to come here, without your kids." They did, immediately.

I called Mark's dad, who also got into his car in Dallas without delay and headed to Austin.

By this time, Bill Jones had arrived and was communicating with the state troopers from our house. He stepped in and out the front door, taking calls and answering questions about the search.

Soon after six o'clock, Bill stepped back through the front door and walked straight to me.

He clasped my face in his hands and took two full breaths before he could say the words. "Becky, Mark is dead."

"No! No! No!" I screamed and thrashed. Bill held firm. "Maybe he's not dead yet," I whimpered, because there was no air to fuel another scream.

"No, Becky, Mark is dead."

Kathy Smith recalls my phone crashing to the wood floor. The echoing thud startled her. I remember only the feeling of all the air being pulled from me. I couldn't breathe. I was in a vacuum and, as the last air was pulled, it drew a deep moan and I fainted. Bill caught me.

Although many aspects of that night remain a blur, some details are etched so sharply, they'll haunt me forever. Bill carried me to my bed, where I woke minutes later. I leaped up. The kids weren't home yet and they couldn't find me there. They couldn't see me in bed; I needed to be strong. This first instinct, to lead and protect my kids, kicked in that moment and stayed with me until . . . Well, like any mother, it lingers still.

By this time, as I learned the details of Mark's death, friends had called friends, and my house was full. Others had to tell me later who was there. It took prompting and time to remember some of those details. But I can still see Madison, Boone, and my nephew Joey coming home from the movie around seven o'clock. Madison quipped softly to Joey and Boone as they walked up the front walk, "Mom and her parties...someone's always here."

I can still hear them laugh and joke as they made their way into the living room about some motorcyclist doing wheelies on the street during their drive home.

Within a few steps they noticed the living room's silence and shot their attention to me. "Mom?"

I focused on Madison as I crossed the room. How do you tell a twenty-year-old girl her dad is dead? I glanced to Boone. How do you tell an eighteen-year-old boy about to graduate from high school, the very image of his father, that his dad has taken his own life and he is now the man of the family? The grief was crushing.

When we were close and touching, I simply said, "Your father is not alive." I had no other words.

Madison immediately said, "What happened?"

I told her Mark had shot himself. Even if I had wanted to lie to protect her, the truth would come out soon enough.

We tumbled into each other's arms and held tight, until their questions began. *Where? When? Why?*

Madison kept shaking her head with each answer. "No. No. No." Again and again, she repeated the word, just as I had, trying to rewrite what I had told them, trying to make it not true.

Within minutes, Kathy Smith heard her cry out, "Who's going to walk me down the aisle?"

A commotion drew my attention to the door. Through the windows everyone could see John Luke and Jackson approaching the house. Bill stepped outside and paused with Jackson to allow John Luke to enter alone.

John Luke's face paled as he took in the scene. Madison, Boone, and I immediately surrounded him. I barely got the same five words out before he broke away from us and ran to the stairs. I raced after him as others consoled Madison and Boone.

John Luke threw himself on his bed, sobbing. I dropped next to him and held him tight. We stayed like that for a long time. He didn't ask any questions. I didn't offer any answers. He simply cried and I held him, tearless. Already, without consciously determining it, I was ordering my responses, my way to get through this, my way to guide my children. There would be tears, more of them than I thought humanly possible, but not at that moment.

While I was upstairs, a good friend, Brian Crowell, took his son and Boone out to our back patio for a private talk. He told both boys, as his son BJ didn't know, that his own father had committed suicide and he understood exactly what Boone was going through and would go through. Right away, Brian and others began to surround my children with love.

Later John Luke and I joined the others in the living room. He sat with his siblings while I took in all the friends who had arrived: the Jameses, the Wises, the Adamses, the Gonzaleses, the Rays, the Timmermans, the Baselices, the Crowells, the Howells, Kathy Smith, and Suzanne Bell, they were all there—along with at least thirty other people.

Suzanne had arrived after seeing a post on Facebook. While I was with John Luke, Madison had posted a picture of Mark with the caption "Rest in peace, Daddy. I love you."

Suzanne texted her: That's not funny, Madison. Take that down immediately.

Had Suzanne known the truth, she wouldn't have sent her that text. However, she had thought Madison's post was an odd joke, until Kathy Smith called her moments later.

I did not see the Facebook post, but several of my friends saw it right away and asked Madison to delete it. It was another moment of misunderstanding between the generations. While we make calls, their generation reaches out and posts on social media sites. Madison did nothing wrong. In her grief, she was reaching out to friends in honesty and vulnerability—and was chided for it. She erased the post within minutes, but, in the end, it proved far more effective at letting friends know of Mark's death than did our phone calls.

Soon my sister Mary Beth arrived. She hugged me and then, being ten years older, took my phone and took charge. She managed the incoming calls and only handed the phone to me when a close friend was on the line. Dinah, the friend who had missed our usual lunch that very day, called from her layover in London.

"I just talked to Kathy. We're coming back."

I'm sure the call was longer than that, but I don't remember anything more we said. It was eleven o'clock and I was numb. My phone pinged with an email from Julie Crenshaw:

Becky,

Ben and I heard a rumor that Mark passed away and he drove to your home and said there are a bunch of cars. He didn't want to intrude especially since we have little info. All I know is our family is praying for your family.

Can we come see you tomorrow? We want to respect your wishes and I think my Ben just wants to hug your boys and tell them how much he enjoyed his friendship and what a great father he was. We've always been so impressed with his devotion.

Becky, please know how much I care for you and have always loved that we met our guys at the same time. I'm here to help, mainly just to be your friend and comfort you.

Love
Julie

Mary Beth reclaimed my phone to continue calling both sides of my family and close friends from my contact list.

It was then that Bill Jones and Monte James, both law-yers, began asking me questions...But something...I needed to remember something...*The file*. Mark had said, "I've left a folder for you in your closet, on the top shelf. You need to follow the instructions exactly." I reached for Bill's hand, tugging him to my bath-room, through which we would reach my closet. Monte followed, and both stopped at the door. Bill pulled me back.

"We can't go in there, Becky. You need to hire us. If you don't, we can't see that file and help you."

Help me?

Bill lowered his voice as if talking to a small child. "Pay us something. Hire us as your legal counsel."

Monte looked to Bill, then to me. "Mark called me, Becky, but this is your decision. You don't know me as well as you know Bill. You don't have to hire me."

Monte and I had met only a couple of times. Bill had been a close friend for years—a close friend to Mark and to me. He was also a close friend of Monte's, and that was enough for me. I grabbed two hundred-dollar bills from my underwear drawer.

Monte pressed it back into my hands. "Becky, give me a twenty. You will need the money."

With twenty dollars each, I hired Bill Jones and Monte James as my personal attorneys. For what, I had no idea.

Then we pulled down the file. It was three inches thick and it contained...*everything*.

Mark had written his obituary, arranged his funeral, outlined our club memberships and expenses, and listed our investments and accounts. He'd made a financial statement of all our assets and liabilities. He'd highlighted our insurance policies and enclosed their statements. Most of them dated back twenty years. The number and amounts of the policies, more than fifteen million dollars, surprised both Bill and Monte, but not me. Mark had always believed life insurance was a good investment.

We paged through the folder and found another list Mark left—a long list of people and some banks to whom we owed money. This shocked me. It was extremely long and delineated a lot of money. There was a note attached to it and a copy of the same Atlantic Trust indemnity clause he'd emailed to Monte. The note instructed me *not* to use the insurance money to repay the people on the list. Mark outlined that I was to keep the insurance money for the kids and me and let Atlantic Trust repay the people he owed from their insurance policy.

"Oh, my gosh…what is this?" I handed the list and the note to Bill. I glanced at the Atlantic Trust indemnity brochure, then handed that to him as well. He scanned all of it, turning through the pages, and handed each to Monte as he finished. Monte focused on the pages as well. Neither spoke.

For what felt like an eternity, but was probably only several seconds, I waited. When no one spoke, I probed again. "What is this?"

Bill stared at me. "It's a bloodbath. That's what this is."

"He told me to keep this money? This insurance money? And we owe people? How do we owe anybody? Is he serious?"

"This is very serious," Monte said.

"I am not keeping any money. If we owe people, we need to pay them back." Without words or coherent thoughts, I handed him the entire folder.

"We need to take all the guns out of the house. It's the right thing to do," Bill said as Monte handed him the pages he held.

I glanced around, thinking of the guns in our house and the reality that Mark had shot himself. "Of course, take them all."

Bill and Monte went to gather the guns, and there were many—after all, this was Texas.

I returned to my kids. They were exhausted and had piled into my bed with Melissa Howell, a dear family friend. Our family doctors, Kevin and Barrie Spencer, were in the house and told me it was important we all stay together. I wanted that, too. I couldn't bear for any of us to be alone. The kids decided they wanted to sleep in Boone's room together in the twin beds with an air mattress for John Luke on the floor. But I couldn't agree. Although John Luke wanted to be with them, I couldn't let him go. He was the youngest and, at that moment, felt the most vulnerable—or maybe I was the most vulnerable. Rather than let him go with his siblings, I insisted he stay with me. John Luke stayed in my bed as the others went upstairs. Mary Beth kept him company. I needed to talk to and sit with Mark's father, Boomer, who had driven from Dallas and arrived shortly before midnight. I also needed to talk with Jeff Stedman, Mark's best friend from Colorado Springs, whom I had called right after talking to Mark. He had flown in from Denver and was expected at any moment.

At three a.m., Mary Beth and I traded places.

At six a.m., after only three hours of sleep, I woke to a gunshot. It was deafening, precise, and painful. Only a dream—but terrifying.

I knew life would never be the same.

Chapter 3

I've been watching you, Dad, ain't that cool?...I wanna
be like you...

—"Watching You" by Rodney Atkins

It is overwhelming to try to unravel the past, deal with
the present, and anticipate the future. All three hit me
hard that next morning. And I wasn't equipped for it.
None of us are, not to mention that, to a great degree, it's
impossible to be. I had the ability to face each moment
only as it came and trust God to meet me there.

Friday started earlier than Thursday had—and after
only three hours of sleep. The shot that woke me felt
so real. I can still hear it; I can still feel it. I crawled
out of bed and left John Luke sleeping. After asking
my brother-in-law Johnny to sit with him so John Luke
wouldn't wake alone, I grabbed my Bible to sit in Mark's
study. This was where I felt his presence most in our
home. This was where I felt most comfortable. Over the

next few days, this was primarily where friends found me, sitting in a corner of the leather sofa, my Bible clutched in my hands, trying to make sense of the world around me.

That morning, I started a ritual that would last for months. I woke early, before anyone else in the house; I curled into a corner of the brown sofa and began paging through my Bible. I couldn't read at any length from that first morning on. I couldn't concentrate. My head spun—as it did for many months—so I found myself reading snippets of the Psalms. I'll tell you, Psalms is a great book for one who feels like she's drowning. My favorite is Psalm 34: *I sought the Lord, and he answered me; he delivered me from all my fears* (v 4). Psalm 46:1 brought immediate comfort, too. *God is our refuge and strength, an ever-present help in trouble.*

Our neighbor Mike Baselice also started a ritual that morning that he continued for months. Also an early morning person, after his daily Starbucks run, he would grab my newspaper—until I canceled it days later—on his way up the drive. But even without a paper, he would check in for a few moments, then proceed through the gate we'd built into our backyard fence years before to return to his house.

While sipping coffee and praying in Mark's study that morning, I found the house had filled again. Many who came the night before had stayed over, and more friends and family arrived from out of town. My parents and my brother Johnny (warning: There are lots of Johnnys in my life and in this story) and his son also drove in that morning.

My dad hugged me long and hard when he stepped inside the door, and for months he could not look at me without tears in his eyes. Even though it was too hard to talk to my parents about what was going on, they'd always given me unconditional love. To have that steadfast love right there, present in the house, holding me tight, brought a tangible peace.

A couple of the earliest arrivals that morning were my friends who now became my lawyers, Monte James and Bill Jones. My daily briefings and questioning began in earnest. The SEC had already contacted Atlantic Trust, and rumors about Mark's death and a large amount of money borrowed began to spread locally like wildfire. Monte said we needed to be prepared for anything.

"Anything? What does that mean? I don't know anything. I didn't do anything," I said. I clutched my Bible in my lap.

"We know that." Bill dropped into Mark's desk chair and rolled it over. He laid a hand on mine until I gave him my full attention. "But they don't. We have to be smart. We have to find answers as soon as possible."

Monte stood beside us, laying out first steps. "It's extremely important, should you be approached by anyone, the press, the FBI, creditors...you say nothing. You talk to us first. Don't destroy anything, don't talk to anyone about this, and shut down all social media accounts."

"What? The FBI? Why did you say that?"

"There will be a criminal investigation, Becky." He faced me. "They'll be involved and they'll want to talk to you."

"But I didn't do anything. Why would they want to talk to me?"

"At some point they will. Now we need to ask you about some of these accounts Mark listed."

We canvassed the banks Mark and I used and the banks on his list—some of which I knew nothing about. They also asked me to open a checking account with a banker I trusted and to withdraw cash from my current account.

"Am I to close the account I've used?"

"No. You are to leave everything as it is. We'll record your withdrawal and everything you do, but you're going to need to pay bills and buy groceries. You simply need your own account now and, if your accounts are frozen, you'll need some cash to live on until this gets sorted."

Soon they left to find Madison and Boone to give them a version of what was going on, and to supervise shutting down all their social media accounts. John Luke was excluded since he had no social media accounts and I felt he was too young to be part of that conversation.

Bill later told me their talk was short and to the point. He simply told the kids, "Your mom is overwhelmed right now. This is a very serious problem we're dealing with and we need you two to grow up fast and help her out. There are things we can't tell you, things she can't tell you, and you're going to have to be okay with that. It's a lot to ask, but I need you to trust me."

He instructed them to immediately shut down their Facebook accounts and any other forms of social media. This was imperative because, as we had learned the night before, social media spreads news fast, real or fake. In fact, in the hours between Mark's death and when Madison deleted her Instagram account, she received more than 200 new followers. It was exactly what my lawyers expected and why they wanted my family's public profile diminished as soon as possible and as much as possible. They wanted to stop anyone searching for information—the press, creditors, or anyone investigating Mark or us.

In order to describe what Bill did next I need to lay something out. Bill is African American.

After instructing my two eldest to delete all social media, he found the boy Madison was dating in the house to talk to him as well. After advising him not to post anything on social media, Bill turned into the protective dad Madison had just lost. "I need you to know I'm Madison's black daddy now. I don't want to get involved in your stuff, but if I have to get involved, I'm going to get all up in there and it won't be pretty. Do you understand?"

The boy was speechless.

My kids trusted Bill. I also believe his "black daddy" comment gave Madison the sense of security that had been ripped from her the day before. His talk with them didn't stop their questions. How could it? But it laid the foundation for some understanding between us when Bill or I would shake our heads and say, "We can't talk about that."

While Bill and Monte talked with Madison and Boone that morning, I grabbed my phone and called Eddie Safady, the president of Prosperity Bank and another good friend. I asked him to come over immediately.

Within what felt like a few minutes, I spied him through our street-facing windows. I ran across the living room and, according to him, met him at the front door and hauled him into the study and shut the door behind us. I have to take his word for that, since I have no memory of it. In fact, much of what I write about these early days is cloudy and was made clear only after talking to friends.

"I'm hearing all these things. I'm hearing we owe people twenty million dollars," I said, crying and shaking.

Eddie tried to calm me down. Mark had approached his bank for a loan, so he knew only that part of the puzzle. When Eddie's bank turned Mark down, Eddie suspected he had gone elsewhere, but never for as much as the number I threw out. Eddie later confessed his shock to me. He thought the amount of Mark's debt was going to be a tenth of what I had suggested.

"Don't worry," he said at the time. "We'll figure it all out."

He calmed me with reassurances we both knew weren't true. It hadn't been twenty-four hours since Mark's death, and rumors were already reaching me, rumors of money borrowed, money missing, friendships abused, and friends duped. People wanted to know where their money had gone, how much had been lost or spent, and whether or not I had known. Everyone also wanted to know what I was going to do.

"I need to open an account with you," I told Eddie. "They want me to have one in my own name."

"Of course."

That's how Eddie, a trusted friend with a birthday ten days from mine, became my banker.

While the lawyers and I handled these first steps, friends handled everything else. My sister Mary Beth kept my phone and contacted all my friends as well as the funeral home. She scheduled an appointment for the next day. Melissa Howell started to unwind and obtain refunds for Madison's Italian semester, and went shopping for the kids' funeral clothes. She also shut down any superfluous avenues of spending. We knew right away that there was going to be no money left. We also canceled our newspaper subscriptions—not because they were expensive but because I didn't want the kids seeing the news in the coming days.

Bill and Monte also reached out to Jeff Stedman that morning to discuss how to get me out of the house fairly quickly. It was too large, and now much too expensive. They didn't want to overwhelm me, but were concerned about how I would pay for the house, or even handle the logistics of moving, so they turned to Mark's best friend.

Because most of the people on Mark's list were friends and acquaintances, word had also begun to circulate that I'd hired Bill and Monte as my lawyers. Creditors were already calling them to ask when and how they would be repaid. We didn't know the extent of what Mark owed, but we knew it was a lot from the list he had left. But now came rumors of other loans, of more money, and of lawsuits. In fact, by Monday, four days after Mark's death, the first lawsuit against Mark's estate was filed with the courts.

Bill and Monte knew repaying the loans was not going to be a cut-and-dried affair despite the fact that I wanted to do just that, not wanting to keep any of the money from Mark's insurance policies. They also knew that because Mark had been a financial planner, the SEC and other federal agencies would be involved. And the fact that Mark's list of creditors was a "Who's Who" of Texas only compounded the problems.

They anticipated publicity, lawsuits, and potential criminal charges. Unbeknownst to me, within twenty-four hours of Mark's death, Monte and Bill began looking for a probate attorney, a tax attorney, a bankruptcy attorney, and had already consulted a criminal attorney. In fact, the criminal attorney was the author behind Monte's statement to me not to destroy anything and not to speak to anyone, and to get rid of social media. In a case with that much money involved, the criminal attorney had told him, "Someone is going to have to pay, and someone is going to jail."

The understanding that Mark wanted me to keep the insurance money, and that he assumed I would, hit me very hard. As much as I now felt I didn't know my husband, he obviously didn't know me. First Timothy 6:10 came to mind repeatedly in those early moments after I opened that file: *For the love of money is a root of all kinds of evil. Some people, eager for money, have wandered from the faith and pierced themselves with many griefs.*

We were certainly grieving and, from my perspective, the love of money had gotten us into a horrible mess. And while supplying us with money had undoubtedly been one of Mark's motivations in taking his life, money was never going to free us. Furthermore, the money from the insurance policies felt dirty to me. In my mind, it wasn't ours. Someone else had paid for our lifestyle, for every trip we took, for Madison's debutante balls, for our Christmas parties, for every charitable contribution, for our clothing—for every single aspect of our lives. To not pay them back meant they'd still be paying for our lives—for the rest of our lives.

Even our memories didn't feel like ours to keep.

I had one goal. It drove each and every conversation in those early days with Bill and Monte. "When can we pay people back?"

Once they'd talked to the kids about their social media accounts and returned to Mark's study, we started again. "When can we pay people back?"

"We don't know anything yet, Becky. We need some time. You focus on Mark's funeral and we'll get to this afterward." Bill sat with me for hours that Friday afternoon. "But..."

"But what?"

"We don't know what we're dealing with and, to be honest, it's moving fast. You have to be prepared for anything, Becky, even another family."

That statement stopped me in my tracks. It still haunts me. It never materialized, but the fact that Bill felt the need to warn me is telling. No one had any idea how deep or wide Mark's world went.

When I wasn't in the study, I drifted through the house. It was full of friends and family—so many kind people pouring love on my kids and me. Kathy Smith had brought her famous cinnamon rolls that morning. Melissa and her husband, Ben, ran my house and took care of odd jobs. Dinah, just arrived from her London flight home, gave me a long hug and started protecting me. As the gossip rolled and the stories gave life to speculation, Dinah shut it down. Leslie did, too. And Jill, Christie, and Chrissy filled the house with kids, which was exactly the distraction my kids needed. It kept the questions and the hurt at bay.

That night before turning in, I wanted to see and kiss each of my kids one last time. The house was still so full of their friends and people; it didn't surprise me when I had to push at Boone's bedroom door to enter. Kids sprawled across his floor. What did surprise me was the half-full bottle of tequila resting on the bedside table.

I lost it.

I grabbed the bottle, yelling at the entire group, "This is not how we're going to handle this!" I ran from the room livid, and I can still feel that visceral anger and that fear. Mark had battled addiction for years and, in that moment, I became terrified this was the beginning of that road for my kids. Without thinking I dashed to the only empty room I could find, the laundry room. There I threw the bottle as far and hard as I could, screaming as loud and long as I could. I was lucky it was plastic and didn't shatter. It bounced off the cabinet and thudded to the floor. My focus on my kids became laser-like as I watched the bottle roll across the floor. The road ahead of us was going to be hard and long, and they needed to trust in and rely on God and turn to me as a guide, not to alcohol or anything else.

Once I calmed down, I found each of my kids and led them to my bedroom. Their friends had scattered to other parts of the house.

We climbed onto my bed, and I laid it out for them as best I could: "We aren't going to handle this with alcohol. Do you hear me? Not at all. We aren't going to be victims. This is hard, really hard, but we're going to make it. And right now, we can't forget that everyone is looking at us. They are watching everything we do, everything we say, and every penny we spend. You've heard the rumors and, while I don't know what we're up against, I do know that alcohol and 'woe is me' aren't going to get us through this. We can't escape the pain that way. Alcohol is not going to be the solution. We have to be there for each other and we have to trust God to see us through. It's all we can do."

They said little. What could they say? All any of us wanted to do was cry. I told them again it was going to be hard, beyond hard, but sharing with each other and talking about all the feelings that would assault us would help. We couldn't hide from any of it or we'd blow up. They nodded their heads again and again, and then we did the only thing we could—we cried, again.

Before falling asleep that night, I made three resolutions:

1. Get up and shower every day.
2. Put on my makeup.
3. No drinking.

These resolutions were for my kids. They were, of course, for me, too, but I was focused on my three. They needed to see me facing this mess head-on. And even if the makeup got cried off every day, there was a certain battle cry in putting it on daily, too. That's what I wanted them to see in me.

The last was about what I didn't want them to see in me . . . I love red wine and have a particular adoration for champagne. I love the social aspect of wine as well. Friends often came over in the late afternoon and evenings for a glass or two and we'd sit and talk, first in a section of our basement I'd converted into a wine cellar, then up in the kitchen as I made dinner. But there was also a reason why I love wine and Joe Nichols's song "Tequila Makes Her Clothes Fall Off." There is a seductive aspect to wine and drinking that softens reality.

I needed to see reality in all its hardness with all its sharp edges—no matter how tough it got. I needed a clear head to walk the road we'd been placed upon. I needed to *be alert and of sober mind* (1 Peter 5:8). I needed my clothes to stay on.

I began each day with Rules 1 and 2, and Rule 3 governed my evenings. I started another ritual that first night as well, one that became so vital to my daily life it should have been on my list of rules. After the makeup was all cried off and I was too tired to lift my head, I listened to country music. The music—with all its heartbreak, pain, and hope—lifted me up again during my nightly bubble bath.

That second night I slept.

Chapter 4

Wish I didn't know now what I didn't know then...

—"Wish I Didn't Know Now" by Toby Keith

The next morning, Mary Beth's husband, Johnny, knocked on the study door. "We need to go."

"Okay." I closed my Bible.

First Johnny was accompanying me to Chase Bank to withdraw cash, as Monte and Bill had advised. I was scared. I didn't know if I was going to have to sign papers; I didn't know if the accounts had been frozen; I didn't know if I'd be watched, detained, or even stopped. I was scared someone would see me and think I was running. And I felt guilty for taking money out, or for needing it at all. But I also trusted Bill and Monte— and I knew we needed something to live on.

After the bank visit—which went smoothly—Johnny headed west a hundred miles outside Austin to pick up

Mark's car from the county in which he died. It had been released by the police. I, along with Mary Beth and our friend and pastor Mark Adams, headed south to the funeral home to plan the funeral.

Mark had arranged his own funeral at Weed-Corley-Fish Funeral Home on the far south side of Austin, an area in which no one would recognize him. He enclosed the funeral home's brochure as well as information for the cemetery in his folder. To walk into that funeral home and, at forty-seven, plan my husband's funeral was physically painful. Yes, I was overwhelmed and not processing much, but to be in that place going over the logistics that Mark himself had planned was devastating.

He also left specific instructions for no public service.

"I can't do that to my kids. We are not going to hide. We did nothing wrong, and I don't want them to feel ashamed. It's already too hard for them. Mark needs a public service. He led a public life." Despite my words, I felt divided. It *was* Mark's request.

Mary Beth squeezed my hand. "I think Mark lost his vote on this one. You plan what you want."

She was right.

We sat down with an older woman who recited the list of all Mark had purchased, part of the funeral home's "full package." It included an unbelievable number of items—necklaces and memory cards, a metal liner for the casket with pictures etched on top, cheese and crackers at the viewing, and a four-color trifold program.

"I don't want all this."

The woman sat straighter. I got the sense she had planned hundreds of funerals, and I was taking her off script. She said in a kind voice, "But you paid for all this." She slid an example of the four-color trifold program across the table.

"Please." I shook my head and pushed it back in her direction. "I don't want any of it. Not even a color program."

She wasn't hearing me. "This is what you've paid for. Your package includes this brochure and all these things."

Panic rose within me. I wanted a simple, understated service. After all, everyone was watching everything we did and the money we spent. I didn't want any-one commenting that Mark's service was elaborate or extravagant.

She opened her mouth to add something more when I lifted a hand. "Just give me a plain eight-and-a-half by eleven sheet of paper."

Mark Adams and Mary Beth sat silent beside me until she returned with a single sheet of copy paper. I folded it in half. "I want this. In ecru. With black print."

Surprised and clearly displeased, she wrote down my request. "But, of course, you want the cheese and crackers."

I felt rather than saw Mary Beth and Mark pass a look over my head. They both knew me. I had never served cheese and crackers at an event in my life, much less for my husband's viewing. They wondered what I was going to do and, for a heartbeat, so did I. I was so close to losing it right then and there. "Are you kidding me? No. I don't want cheese and crackers. No, thank you."

Mary Beth and Mark burst out laughing. Soon we three were laughing. The woman was not. I think I insulted her, but I also don't think she understood all that was going on. I was beyond myself at that point, and the flash of laughter cut the tension and let me regain a little perspective.

Which I lost in the next moment...

As the meeting wrapped up, the manager came over. "I'm so sorry...I met your husband a few days ago."

I almost choked. It gave my husband's visit context and a date, and it gave me a visual. I wondered if I thought hard enough, could I remember what he wore that day, what we said at dinner that night? He had been in this place, arranging these details only days before.

The manager spoke across my runaway thoughts. "We always wonder when people that young come in. I asked him why, and he said he'd recently traveled to Mexico and had a little scare. It made him want to have everything taken care of."

Mary Beth saw my face and acted instantly. She took my arm—the meeting was over. I stumbled over a goodbye and thank you, and we left.

In the end, there were few of Mark's plans I chose to keep. I wanted a simple and open ceremony that would allow friends and family to say goodbye.

One detail I didn't catch and decline, however, was the forty-page, photographic commemorative book. It arrived in the mail five months later—another perk of the "full package."

Upon arriving home that afternoon, I found the police had not only released Mark's car but also his personal effects. Johnny handed me a large manila envelope containing Mark's wedding ring, his watch, and several letters. Mark had left handwritten notes for each of our children. Mark loved to write and had often left us notes. In fact it was one of the first things Madison had cried out on Thursday night. "There has to be a letter. Dad wouldn't leave without a letter."

Now my kids read their father's last words to them.

Each letter was personal, but they held common elements. He expressed his shame and regret to all three kids, then pleaded with each to "be 100% honest with everybody about everything all the time and pursue God." He underlined "pursue" in all three letters. He then closed his loving words with "I can't wait to see you in heaven...in about seventy-five years."

The letters brought and still bring each of my kids comfort. In fact, it wasn't until I started pulling together thoughts for this manuscript that the kids read each other's letters. For five years, they had held their letters close and private. I think it brought another moment of healing when they recently shared them and further understood their collective journey.

But Saturday didn't end there...That night Boone

dressed for his senior prom. He didn't want to let his
date down, so he put on the tuxedo and accompanied
her to the pre-dance party for pictures. His friends then
took over and escorted her to dinner and to the dance.
It was hard, and felt very surreal to take pictures of a
smiling Boone dressed up to celebrate. Yet I couldn't
help smiling. I was so proud of him for thinking of
his date that night. But emotions didn't feel easy and
pure in those early days. Laughter always blended with
sorrow. It hurt that this night wasn't one of celebration
for Boone, and it hurt that it was merely the third of a
lifetime of hard nights and coping with loss. And beyond
the loss, there was an extra burden Boone carried, all
my children carried. We heard the questions and felt
the stares. Even when people were "for us," it was hard
not to assume they were "against us." Boone felt it all
that night.

Bill and Monte sat me down the following afternoon, again in Mark's study. While I had followed
Bill's advice and spent my Saturday focused on Mark's
funeral and my kids, he and Monte had spent their
Saturday fielding calls from Invesco, Atlantic Trust's
parent company, creditors, the Department of Justice,
the SEC, and the FBI. There were now things to
discuss that could not wait until after the funeral. The
first item they mentioned was that the papers planned
to break the story the next day. Mark's suicide and
financial dealings, and speculation over what might
happen next, would appear over the next several weeks

and months in the *Austin American-Statesman* as well as other Texas and national media, including the *Wall Street Journal* and a segment on CNBC.

Bill looked out the window to the street. We expected the press to descend upon us at any moment. "The media coverage will only increase, Becky. This is big."

"What does that mean?"

This time Monte rolled the desk chair to me. "It means this is of national interest. We've probably got three to five years of litigation ahead of us. There will be lawsuits; you'll need to file for bankruptcy, and there are tax implications to all this we can't even anticipate. We've also hired you a criminal attorney."

"What? Why?" I jumped off the sofa. "Why would you do that? I didn't do anything."

"It's getting more complicated."

"How complicated?" I dropped back down.

"Complicated enough to keep you all off social media, to keep the news outlets interested and coming around, and to send you to jail."

That dropped my head to my hands. Never once did I think I'd be in trouble. I thought we'd have no money, and the shadow of bankruptcy had crossed my mind. But...*jail*? That had not occurred to me. "I want to pay everyone back. I have the life insurance money and the house. We can sell everything if we have to and give it all to the creditors."

"It's not that simple."

"Then explain it to me."

They laid out the criminal aspects of the case, which were so serious that not only had they hired me a criminal attorney, but they'd also hired Johnny Sutton, the former United States Attorney for the Western District of Texas, one of the largest and busiest districts in the United States. Furthermore, they had kept the hiring of Johnny confidential because once creditors heard his name, panic and lawsuits might ensue. I gathered such a big legal gun signaled there was a lot at stake.

Bill and Monte shared a long look before Monte turned back to me. "One more thing. Johnny has advised us not to tell you anything you don't already know." He held up his hand to stop me from interrupting. "The FBI will interview you, Becky, and you need clarity about what you knew and when you knew it. He's also the one who said not to delete or destroy anything. Not a bank statement, not even an email. You throw out nothing. Do you understand?"

I nodded. The meeting ended, and I went out into the living room, where friends and family gathered.

Later that afternoon, when I had a moment to sit down, I joined Lisa Stedman and Mary Beth in my bedroom. I dropped onto the bed, exhausted and in pain. My shoulders, where I hold my tension, were so tight they hurt to move or touch. I pressed my hand to my chest.

"Becky?" Mary Beth leaned toward me.

"I can't breathe. I can't draw a breath." It felt as if a vise were crushing my chest.

Someone called Barrie Spencer, our family doctor, who had been at the house on and off all weekend. She came immediately, and we sat alone in my bedroom. After a few minutes of examination, she sat holding my hand. "You're having a panic attack."

"But I don't feel panicked."

"Your body can absorb panic in a lot of ways. Are you eating?"

"Mary Beth and Melissa keep shoving food at me."

She raised a brow.

"It's going straight through me. There's nothing I can do about that."

"Becky, look, you're under tremendous pressure right now. You have to get rest and figure out how to release this tension. You need to be there for the kids now and for months ahead. You need your strength."

Looking back, I think Barrie knew—as so many on the outside did—what I was facing better than I did. I was still too overwhelmed to process much.

We talked further, and she recommended an anti-anxiety pill and Ambien to help me sleep. "I think you should have these on hand when you need them. You don't want to get run-down and sick. Rest and sleep will help prevent that. It's important right now. You may also find the anti-anxiety medication helps the day of the funeral. It's going to be hard."

She wrote out the two prescriptions, which Melissa went to fill for me—since I had another difficult conversation ahead.

Telling my children their dad died was and, I firmly believe, will always be my hardest moment. To withstand something horrible and painful is one thing, but to know your kids must endure it is another. With that in mind, my heart hurt so much for my parents and for Mark's parents. It was surreal to tell them that I could go to jail for Mark's actions and that I needed their help to pay my criminal attorney's $50,000 retainer and another attorney's $20,000 retainer. My parents said, "Whatever you need," and asked no questions. Then I told Boomer, who sat silent and stoic. I could tell he was already trying to fix the situation. Even though Peggy, Mark's mom, was not there, I knew she was praying for all of us.

In that moment, things shifted within me. I'd lost my husband, my kids had lost their father, the future was going to be hard financially—but through all that, we could be okay. Yet as I articulated my need for a criminal attorney and spoke aloud the reality that I could go to jail for something I didn't know was going on, that I might be taken from my kids to pay for my husband's actions, and that my kids could lose both their parents, a swell of incredulous anger rose within me. Furthermore, I was three days into this ordeal and had already spent more than $100,000 in attorney retainer fees with no clue how it would end.

After my bubble bath the next night, the night before Mark's funeral, I took half an Ambien pill. Even though I'd been sleeping soundly, I worried that this night might derail me. I was anxious about Mark's service and the magnitude of the next day. Within twenty minutes, I didn't feel like myself, and my panic grew. I am not giving an opinion on anyone else's journey, only my own. I felt the medication move into me as decisively as if someone flipped a switch. I felt distanced from myself, and I knew it wasn't for me. Medication can do amazing good and should always be taken when needed. But for me, it felt as if I was making an active choice to step back from my reality. I couldn't do that. I needed to be aware, *of sober mind*, including all of my flaws and failures. I took both bottles and threw the medications away.

My house remained full for the days before Mark's funeral with friends who loved us and protected us in many ways. But the tension of all we faced built, and by Monday, my shoulders were so tight I couldn't sit straight or even hold myself upright when standing. Lisa rushed out to bring me a neck-massaging wrap. Knowing I was having a hard time accepting all the help given to me, even this early on, she lied and claimed, "It was a gift with purchase." I accepted the "gift with purchase" and spent hours wrapped within its heated coils before I could sit straight or move with any comfort. And every time I did turn those few degrees, a friend was gently pushing food toward me or suggesting I rest. And when the kids emerged from alone time in their rooms, which they craved periodically, I felt the need to put eyes on them and make sure each was okay. I felt so grateful the kids didn't push me away or get irritated with my hovering, despite their being far too old for it. They confided in me again and again how good it felt to have friends near, to play games or kick a ball around the backyard, or to simply sit and watch a movie. I will be forever thankful that we were not alone those first days. There is no denying that the situation in which we found ourselves invited shame. And the constant love that surrounded us fought that dark shadow.

On Tuesday, May 21, the kids and I didn't need alarms to wake us. Early, I headed to Mark's study. My devotional at the time was *Jesus Calling: 365 Devotions for Kids.* It's a little simpler than the adult version, which was and is good for me. I like things presented simply and plainly. I opened the red cover to the day's page and sat staring. The very passage I had chosen for Mark's funeral, which would start only hours from that moment, was the prescribed and printed reading for the day. Romans 8:28: *And we know that in all things God works for the good of those who love him, who have been called according to his purpose.*

God was clearly telling me: *I am here.*

I had felt it before in my morning prayer time, poring over the Psalms, but it crystallized into those three words that morning. They felt so clear they could have been spoken aloud. *I am here.* I sat marveling at the reading and God's presence and grace, until a shadow crossed the window. I looked up and found another good friend walking across our yard. She wore plastic kitchen gloves and carried a black trash bag.

I ran outside. "What are you doing?"

"Are your dogs here?"

"They're in the laundry room. Melissa is coming to take them to the vet for the day."

"Good. You're going to have hundreds of people here this afternoon. I'm doing the poopectomy."

We had two Newfoundlands. Big dogs. Big poop.

I protested. She insisted. Soon I gave up and returned to the house, and she continued to stroll through our yard clearing it of dog poop. I was astounded by her generosity, just as I had been astounded the day before when the yard crew—the crew I'd let go days before—showed up to plant flowers for free, and another dear friend, Mike Baselice, helped them; and just as I was astounded later that morning when another friend (a creditor, though I didn't know it at that time) brought enough breakfast tacos to feed everyone in the house.

"We'll take care of it," was all any of them said.

Mark's funeral was held on Tuesday, May 21, at Hyde Park Baptist Church. While I had prepared the details for the funeral, turning down more options than accepting them, it was Mike and Julie Baselice who reserved the church and the bagpipe player who later played at the graveside ceremony. I felt our church was too far away to be convenient for most who would want to attend. If I'd considered the logistics of getting to the cemetery along those lines, I might have reconsidered that, too, but we'll get to that in a moment...

More than 1,200 people filled Hyde Park Baptist's sanctuary that afternoon, including Governor and Mrs. Perry and, unbeknownst to me, my new criminal attorney, Johnny Sutton. He later told me he sat in the back to see who was there, hear what was said, and get a feel for the tenor of the creditors.

Boone gave his father a beautiful and moving eulogy, talking about his dog Molly whose loyalty Mark had wooed with tidbits of food under the table and donut holes every Saturday morning. I was so proud of him and his composure and the touching way he spoke of his dad. It was only when he sat down and whispered, "Mom, I can't feel my arms" that I was reminded of the cost of such composure in one so young.

As Boone sat, the memory of his words filled the sanctuary with a lovely silence that celebrated the best of Mark. Then, in a later moment when we all needed a lift, Mary Beth read the emotions perfectly and introduced herself as my "younger" sister. She had played that joke for years and, despite being ten years older than me, had actually convinced my kids when they were young that I was the older one. Her humor brought a much-needed chuckle, and her poignant talk about Mark soothed my soul. Two of Mark's best friends then brought us to tears again, with heartfelt words and fun memories.

Mark Adams spoke last and gave a wonderful sermon

that honored Mark and didn't shy away from suicide. He faced it straight on. I was so thankful. There is an unfortunate stigma of shame surrounding suicide, and surrounding many mental illnesses and struggles, and I didn't want my kids to feel that.

I sat there fairly dry-eyed and was struck by the dawning truth that I could never understand the pain Mark felt nor the depth of his hurt. It became clear in that moment, as Mark Adams addressed the congregation, that I would not and could not get the answers to what had happened within Mark and why. In many ways, God was again saying, *I am here,* because that understanding came with a tremendous sense of peace—which held me together until the final song, "Because He Lives." It brought me to tears.

Mark wished to be buried in a small cemetery in Spicewood, about thirty miles outside Austin. It is a tiny tract of land nestled between two golf courses. It had taken hours and a tremendous effort to locate the owners of Haynie Flat Cemetery, but between Mary Beth and me, we got it done. It was one of Mark's requests I wanted to honor. Golf balls pinged at tees throughout the ceremony, and I understood that was exactly why he'd chosen it.

That said, had I known how long the drive would take from the church to the cemetery, I might have chosen differently. Even though the police shut down Austin's MoPac highway and we drove unimpeded by traffic, the procession was so long it kept the highway closed for half an hour—and that was before the lead car turned and took the most inconvenient route possible, west across Bee Caves Road rather than follow the highway around the heart of Westlake.

I finally leaned forward and tapped the driver on the shoulder. "You have to drive faster. You have to pick up the pace. This is taking forever. It's unbearable."

"Sorry, ma'am. It's the law."

"But I can walk faster." I sat back as my phone lit up. Texts were flying among friends.

The best came from Chrissy Ray: Cole got hungry. We got out of line at Burger King, ordered, and are back in. Can you believe it???

Amid the pain, there was lightness and laughter. Again, no emotion came alone. It was only when the burial ended that a strong shift occurred within me and the love and logistics of the day took a backseat to the loss.

Sobbing, I could not leave Mark's graveside. I couldn't leave him there. It felt too final. I couldn't go. My father let me cry for a time, then gently pulled me away from the casket.

Later that night, after the reception quieted at our home, I gathered with close friends in our basement. The corner I had redecorated a couple years before into a wine cellar for Mark's birthday had become a favorite place of mine. A group of us sat talking about some of the humor that had crept into the day—the "poopectomy" and the Burger King visit ranking highest.

Melissa called me upstairs to the laundry room. She and her husband, Ben, had gone to retrieve our dogs from the vet.

"We have Molly," she said.

I shook my head. Molly was Boone's beagle who had died a couple months before, the one he had alluded to in his eulogy. "You mean you have Maxwell and Griffin."

"No. I mean Molly." Melissa stepped aside. A cedar box and a large plaster plaque with a paw print sat on the counter behind her. "Mark bought the full package, the vet said. There are some trinkets and a set of dog tags, too, but in there..." She pointed to the box. "That's Molly."

I could only laugh. Of course Mark had bought the full package.

Chapter 5

If you're going through hell keep on going, don't
slow down...

—"If You're Going Through Hell" by Rodney Atkins

The battle begins...

"Battle" implies that one must lose for another to
win—and I desperately wanted everyone to win; I
wanted everyone made whole. But it was still a battle.
We were only days in, and my attorneys were already
tired of my questions and my impatience. As I said,
every conversation began with, "When can we pay everyone back?"

On the day of Mark's funeral, American Bank
of Commerce (ABC) sued Mark's employer, Atlantic
Trust, for the $1.1 million Mark owed because he had
used shares of Atlantic Trust securities as collateral.
One creditor had already sued me; and one creditor,
also an attorney, started to create a group of creditors

to represent. It felt as if a union was being formed. I wasn't sure if the "collective bargaining power" of this union was against me or for me. I suspected it was a little of both.

Matthew 7:1 hit home for me in a very real way in these early days. *Do not judge, or you too will be judged.* Jesus was talking about the heart here. He was saying that we don't know other people's hearts. We can judge actions, but we need to be very careful with hearts. People wondered about my heart. *What is she going to do?* was on people's minds and in the air. They were basically asking, *What's in her heart? What does she love?*

Creditors, media, and anyone who knew anything about this situation wondered and often asked their friends—or mine. Many had heard I wanted to pay everyone back and was planning to use the insurance money and sell my house to do so. That led to another question. *Is she really going to do what she says?* One creditor stated it publicly in an *Austin American-Statesman* article published soon after Mark's death: "They're saying there's a bunch of insurance and (Powell's) wife was going to give up everything she had (to repay creditors), but I'll believe it when I see it." So many people felt the same way—they'd believe it when they saw it.

It was made clear to me, the day after Mark's funeral, how long this battle could last and how emotionally draining it would be. On that Wednesday morning, I met my criminal attorney, Johnny Sutton, for the first

time in Monte's office. After all I'd been told about him
and all that lay ahead, I was terrified.

But Johnny was not who captured my attention upon
first entering Monte's conference room, nor did the
familiar faces of Bill or Monte. A lawyer named Frank
Bryan stood directly in front of the door and welcomed
me with a warm smile. I burst into tears. Frank Bryan
was an old friend and is a kind, honest, and trustworthy
man. Johnny, concerned about the size and complexity
of my case, had hired Frank to assist him. In that
moment, without an instant thought, I knew that if
Johnny worked with Frank, I could trust Johnny. Once
again, God was speaking: *I am here.*

Knowing Frank, however, did not make the next four
hours easy. After an initial meet-and-greet, Johnny sat
me down and fired a relentless barrage of questions.
*How was your marriage?...Where did you and Mark
meet?...When?...When did you last quarrel?...Who
handled the finances?* My whole body flushed as the
questions became increasingly personal. At one point,
Monte grew uncomfortable and left the room.

Johnny pressed into every aspect of my life and
marriage, telling me he needed to know "every wart" I
might try to hide. He said he needed to push me to the
brink so that no one was surprised with anything I said
later. He also told me that he had hired a former FBI
agent to search our home; he planned to copy all our
computers' hard drives; and Frank would review all our
bank statements and emails back to 2008. "We aren't

trying to hide anything for you. We're trying to uncover it. We want to know everything the FBI will discover."

He also asked how Mark had more than $15 million in life insurance policies.

"When we got married, one of Mark's friends was in life insurance, and Mark already had several policies. They both saw them as forms of diversification and good investments because they all built up cash values. I got a policy right before our marriage, and each of the kids got policies when they were born."

All Mark's policies were years old. They all had not only long surpassed the two-year suicide exclusion clause, but also the profits of most of the whole life policies had kicked in and were paying their premiums. The existence of the insurance policies didn't surprise me. The fact that Mark had called our estate planning attorney to make sure each was titled into a Powell Family Trust only months before he died did. We canvassed that, too, even though I had no answers.

That meeting was the first of many that week, and the first of countless in the months to come. Throughout the summer, I met with my attorneys almost every day and rarely left the house if it was not to meet with them.

Bill described these early days as "drinking from a fire hydrant." The painful revelations and possible implications hit us so hard and so fast on a daily basis that they demanded almost all our time and attention.

One afternoon, I was called into my probate attorney

Jerry Jones's office to discuss signatures found on some of Mark's documents.

"Is this your signature?" He paged through documents.

Bill had already asked every creditor who called him, "Did you ever talk to Becky about the loan?"

Every single one had replied, "No." Some even said, "Mark told me specifically not to tell her."

Yet here was my name on loan documents.

"That's not mine," I said.

Suddenly I understood that even when forging my signature, Mark had made sure he didn't implicate me. He'd written my name in a swirly script. "I don't write cursive. I never have. I print my signature," I said.

Another day, Mark's insurance representative called for a meeting. Whereas I thought I was signing documents to release the insurance money, he had other plans.

"We aren't anywhere near that point, but I want you to sign these papers to set up an annuity account so when we get there, you'll be prepared. Mark would want this for you, to manage your money. It'll spin out about three million dollars in income annually."

I walked out of that meeting—I had no intention of keeping any of the money.

But it would be dishonest to say that my attorney meetings kept me so busy I couldn't go out in public. Other reasons kept me home. I fought a strong sense of shame and the desire to hide in those early months. It was natural and, though illogical, it was also strong, real, and true. No matter what we're hit with, we want to hide our pain and embarrassment from others. We want to show only our best faces to the world. Social media feeds upon that—everybody makes his or her life look fabulous. That's one of my biggest issues with social media. It sets us up, in many ways, for feelings of shame and failure, because no one posts the bad stuff. It all looks so polished and perfect, and we can never live up to that image.

That was one of the reasons I was pleased my kids were required to shut down their accounts. Johnny had done it for legal reasons, but I couldn't help feeling it also protected their hearts during an incredibly difficult and vulnerable time. Looking at that perfect and polished world on Facebook would have been very hard for them while their world was falling apart; to post their vulnerability and reality would have been impossible. No one does that.

But those concerns—that image of a polished and perfect life—flow into real life as well, and I was hesitant to go out in public. Much of our lives had been paid for by others, and I was afraid people would think I was okay with that, that they would see me out and about having fun, and believe I wasn't taking what Mark had done seriously. I was afraid they would judge my heart and believe the worst of my kids and me. After all, we *had* lived on other people's money.

At home, Melissa continued to handle the day-to-day business of running my life. Mary Beth and Lisa Stedman stayed with me a couple more weeks as well. They, along with a group of dear friends, directed the kids' activities that summer, paid the bills, ordered thank-you notes, organized the meals that friends delivered daily, and picked up every aspect of my previous life. My parents and Mark's parents had left soon after the funeral, but they called every day and made sure to speak with each kid daily, too. So while my kids definitely heard and felt the tensions swirl around us, the constant support of friends and family bolstered them.

Mary Beth even called her contacts in Houston to vet my attorneys and sought out local counselors to meet with my kids. I discovered that counselors didn't necessarily want to meet with my children. One told me that unless I noticed remarkably unusual and concerning behavior, the more ideal time to begin therapy was about a year after a tragedy, since it takes a good deal of time for one to even begin processing that tragedy.

One afternoon in this first week after Mark's death, I returned home from meeting with my lawyers and saw a news van pull up across the street. I ran out as a young man pulled a large camera from the back and hoisted it onto his shoulder. He turned to find me sprinting across the yard. Johnny Sutton had coached me for just this moment.

My outstretched hand turned to offer a handshake as I began to talk. "Please. Please don't film. My kids are here. My attorneys will talk to you. You only have to call them. I'll give you their numbers. Please, you can say anything you want about my husband or me, but please leave my kids out of this. I'm calling my lawyers right now. They'll talk to you."

I dialed Johnny with my free hand. He didn't pick up. I then dialed Bill.

Bill answered. "Give him my phone number. Tell him to call me."

The young man stared at my outstretched hand as I lowered the phone. Then, without another word, he turned and put his camera away, climbed back into his van, and left.

I received a lot of grace in this regard. Media peppered friends and creditors with questions, yet few answered them. Only once was I shocked and hurt by a newspaper story. Early that first week, one article reported private details regarding Mark's death and dealings that only a close friend, present in those moments when I myself learned early truths, could have known. But in today's world where everyone wants his or her "fifteen minutes of fame," to be able to say that happened only once is a miracle. But I know I received this grace only in hindsight. During those early weeks, the fear that the media would show up with the kids around terrified me. I hated all of this for my kids and was so scared they would be questioned, cornered, and hurt.

Fears aside, though, there was work to do, and by the end of the first couple weeks, my entire "team" was assembled. In addition to Bill, Monte, Johnny, and Frank Bryan, Jerry Jones, Al Golden, and Frank Ikard joined as my probate attorneys. Monte and Bill, as my team's quarterbacks, also hired a tax attorney and a bankruptcy lawyer. The last we didn't retain for long because we didn't end up filing for bankruptcy. But early on, I had a "team" of nine. And by the end of the first month, I had paid my team more than $120,000 in billable hours. This set the standard—on average I owed my lawyers about a $100,000 per month.

One of the first things Jerry Jones did when he came on board was put Mark's estate into dependent administration. This meant the court controlled every penny, including the life insurance policies, when and if they paid out. It provided transparency. Every penny moved, spent, or contributed needed court approval, and any lawyer or creditor could access and track the records online.

We knew they were watching, because one afternoon a creditor's attorney called to ask Jerry, "Why isn't the account at Plains Bank listed among her assets?"

Jerry reassured the creditor, through his lawyer, that the balance was zero and therefore the account need not be listed.

In addition to putting the estate into dependent administration, Jerry also put a bond on me. The creditors could now see that not only did I not have access to the money, but I also couldn't "run" anywhere regardless.

During this time, the government agencies—the Department of Justice, the Securities and Exchange Commission, and the Federal Bureau of Investigation—

formally began their investigations. Atlantic Trust, and its parent company Invesco, also began an internal audit. Although my lawyers maintained an open information policy, Invesco initially doubted my desire and ability to repay any creditors, much less all. Their lawyers kept us at arm's length, and communication between them and us was frosty at best, antagonistic at worst.

As of June 3, Invesco reported to my team that 118 creditors were involved and more than $36 million was needed for repayments. The internal audit continued. By June 13, Invesco informed my team the numbers had climbed to 120 creditors and $38.7 million. The forensic accounting team worked on...

I relay these numbers to illustrate how little we knew. Every day new creditors called my lawyers or their own lawyers, who then reached out to mine, with numbers, stories, and often a deep sense of frustration, anger, and betrayal.

These projections devastated me. The goal to pay everyone back every penny borrowed felt unreachable. Such amounts were beyond anything I could repay. Monte tried to balance my perspective and dissuade me from such fanciful thinking. "It never happens, Becky. No one gets whole, ever. A good repayment is ten cents on the dollar."

I asked my lawyers to approach Invesco and ask for assurance that, if I gave all I had, like the widow in the Gospel of Mark who gave her last two cents, they would make up the balance to repay everyone their net

loan amounts. From my perspective, I was saving Invesco millions in both payments and lawsuits, as many
creditors believed the company was liable. I wanted the
commitment that they would back me up if needed.
I couldn't bear to see creditors paid only pennies on
the dollar.

Matthew 22:21 was an important verse for me during
these days. In discussing who is owed what with regard
to a temple tax, Jesus asks listeners whose face is on
the coin in their hands. *"Caesar's," they replied. Then he
said to them, "So give back to Caesar what is Caesar's,
and to God what is God's."* I wanted to give people their
money back, too—every penny of it—to the best of our
collective abilities because it belonged to them. And
by doing that I would give to God what was rightfully
his, my obedience. Unfortunately my lawyers didn't feel
Invesco would agree with my reasoning, and they were
right. But that didn't keep me from asking a few more
times as the numbers climbed.

Beyond the logistics of the money, the very idea of
such an amount shocked me. People had wondered how
the $21 million from Mark's list went "missing." *Was
it "missing"? Had he really spent that much? Was it all
gone?* That was bad enough, but the possibility that the
true number could be $38 million was beyond belief. I
asked myself, *Where did it go?* Boone asked close family
friends the same question. None of us had the answer.
I knew we'd lived an extravagant lifestyle and donated
generously to political campaigns and charities, but

even then I could not reconcile these numbers. Neither could my lawyers.

"You went to the Caymans each spring. Could Mark have an account there?" Monte asked.

"Not that I know of."

He shook his head. "If a safety deposit box key or an account number ever shows up, you have to let me know."

Nothing did or has ever shown up—and I am sure the FBI and SEC searched. I certainly know my lawyers did.

Within days of this conversation, Invesco subpoenaed me for access to all Mark's personal papers and his computer for their forensic accounting investigation. We then subpoenaed them for access to their forensic accounting—which is very expensive—so we didn't have to perform our own.

After all, we wanted the same answers, *and* every penny I saved meant one more for the creditors.

On May 31, we took a significant step forward.

Creditors had begun to file claims against Mark's estate with my lawyers. That is very different from filing a lawsuit against me. A claim means that both parties are working to a resolution; a lawsuit means the court is called in because both parties can't or won't work out a resolution.

Word had gotten around that I was serious in my desire to repay everyone every penny I could. And Bill and Monte made it clear that they would talk to any and all creditors who called their offices with questions. Despite my willingness and my lawyers' open door policy, tensions among creditors grew higher. They knew about the ABC bank lawsuit against Atlantic Trust and they knew about one creditor filing a suit against me.

My lawyers fielded so many calls and questions, they felt pressed to get ahead of the inevitable barrage of lawsuits, the subsequent bankruptcy, and the three to five years of litigation they fully expected. If you read the papers, that's how these cases go. Bernie Madoff's case is the most famous example, but one could fill books with countless others—including the McFarland case that went to trial as I prepared this manuscript. With one suit already filed, creditors saw a diminishing pie in front of them. Any minute we expected a few more to file lawsuits to claim a slice.

Bill suggested calling all the creditors together in one room to outline my intentions. He recently told me, "I sensed the tenor of the creditors. I had made my office available to talk to anyone, and it was about to get really ugly fast."

Every other lawyer balked, but Bill stood firm. He insisted that "laying our cards on the table is the only way forward."

In the end, everyone acquiesced, admitting it might

just be the bold move necessary to keep everything from falling apart.

While planning the May 31 meeting, Monte commented to Bill and Johnny over a conference call that he was going to bring me out at the beginning and tell the creditors I'd answer any and all questions—a definite no-no in the legal world. I gather Bill sputtered a little, and Johnny was so shocked that the line remained silent for a full minute. Neither expected Monte to make light of the situation or to make a joke. Johnny finally replied, "I don't think that's the best idea..."

Needless to say, Monte had not been serious. I was nowhere near his office that day as creditors and their lawyers filed into a conference room. I later learned that as many entered the room, they were surprised with the friends they found there. "You too?"..."He got to you?"..."How'd he convince you?" Shock and questions filled the early minutes.

Mark had approached each man very personally, often relying on years of friendship in making his requests. Even the ones made under "business" auspices had a personal touch. *I've got a great deal going and you're the friend I thought of.* Many requests, however, were far more personal. *I'm a little short on cash and am so embarrassed to even ask this.* It was this idea of exposing one of their own that kept many creditors quiet. They never gossiped about Mark among themselves and none ever shared any of it with me. Looking around the room, the creditors began to understand what we faced and how large a problem was before me. They also saw, with each friend who entered, their chances of seeing their money again slip away.

Bill felt the tension in the room rise and stepped to the front. He explained my intentions to use the proceeds from the insurance policies, from the sale of my home, and from whatever else was necessary to sell, to pay everyone back. He noted that all those assets were protected from their claims upon them, but that I was willingly doing this and had put the estate under dependent administration to show my good faith and intentions. Not only that, but they had put a bond on me as another assurance I was not going to run and I was not going to claim ownership over any of the money.

"We are asking you to remain patient and let us do what we need to do to get everyone the best possible outcome."

Several creditors declared they wanted to sue Invesco, just like ABC bank had, as the company had deeper pockets than I and carried an indemnity policy against employee fraud. Bill raised his hand to caution them and calm the room. He warned that such an action would incite a legal battle that would not only increase their fees but also decimate any chance I had to repay them, as my legal fees would eat up any available money as well. He restated my intention to repay everyone myself, including ABC bank. He then outlined the timeline. Nothing could happen quickly. He said that repeatedly, trying to instill patience into every mind. Invesco hadn't finished its forensic accounting; it had barely started, so final numbers had not been reached. Not only that, but we also still didn't know which insurance policies would pay out. It was a hard ask, but Bill implored every creditor and every lawyer to "stand down" and to wait patiently for me.

"We are doing our best. There are a lot of insurance policies. We don't know if they'll pay, but Becky has put them on the table. She has put everything on the table."

Quiet ensued, and he used the moment to push his point further. "Remember, if the lawsuits start, no one will get paid. You all know how this will go...Years in court and litigation fees will eat up anything you might see. Pennies on the dollar is considered a best outcome in these cases, but we are hoping for better. To that end, everyone must cooperate."

The tenor of the room shifted. He had made his point. He then looked at one man, the one who had sued me the Monday after Mark's death, and asked, "In this spirit, will you withdraw your lawsuit?"

All eyes turned and, whether motivated by embarrassment or peer pressure or God working on his heart, the creditor replied, "Yes."

Another creditor then asked if I was going to keep any of the insurance money or anything at all.

Monte replied, "Not at this time. She doesn't view her 'best interests' as we do. She wants to pay everyone back first. We are hoping to convince her to keep

Mark's retirement accounts to pay bills and to pay her legal fees."

That silenced the room, and the meeting soon ended. One creditor later commented to me, "It was all nice, but we knew the lawyers would never let it happen. All the assets they mentioned were exempt assets, and the lawyers weren't going to let you give it all away. They'd talk you out of it. Nevertheless, we waited. I expected a volley of lawsuits and countersuits, but it never began."

He's right. It never began.

I truly believe God worked in the hearts of a few good men that day, and their example affected the hearts of others, as even the most litigious creditors never sued me.

One lawyer sent Bill a note the next day.

Bill...

I thought you did an excellent job yesterday under very tough conditions. What an incredibly sad situation. However, given that, I think you handled the meeting very well. I hope that Becky can find some peace... someday... after she comes to terms with all this mess. That is more likely to occur with good people and close friends such as yourself.

Creditors didn't file lawsuits, but they kept calling Bill, Monte, and Jerry. Some wanted more details. Some wanted the logistics outlined further. And some wanted to make sure the money wasn't coming from what the kids and I would need to live on. Several even refused to file claims, including Jim Crane, Matt Mathias, and Vaughn Brock, because they didn't want the money to impact the kids and me, and leave us with nothing.

While I was stunned by such care and generosity, I told all of my lawyers to reply with the same message: "She needs everyone to file claims. She needs to repay everyone before she'll think about what comes next. That's what she needs to move forward."

Few creditors approached me directly about the money. But I knew they were talking. Close friends, ones not involved in the financial dealings, would sometimes tell me what they'd heard. Some creditors suspected I'd known all along, some thought I wouldn't sacrifice our lifestyle, some staunchly declared my innocence, and some asked others to stop gossiping.

But one afternoon, someone did reach out to me. A friend of Mark's, a lawyer himself, had drafted a document for one of Mark's first creditors, unaware that the foundational information within the document was false. Mark had then adapted that document for future deals. Now the FBI wanted to interview him. He had called Bill and Johnny, but hadn't heard back. Then he called me.

I listened to his voice mail, and rather than call him back, I called Bill. I took all of my lawyers' warnings very seriously about not talking to anyone about anything.

"I just got this message," I told Bill. "He said he's left messages for you and Johnny, and neither of you have returned his calls. You need to call him back or I will. He's a friend. He's trying to help."

Bill was firm. "We are not going to call him back. We are not going to interfere with a federal investigation."

"But it's rude—"

"You call him back and mess with this investigation, Becky, you will go to jail. And I've seen you in orange. It's not in your color wheel."

Only Bill Jones would say that—and it was enough for me. I did not return the call. But I did send Bill the lyrics from Brandy Clark's "Stripes" a couple days later: "I hate stripes and orange ain't my color...There's no crime of passion worth a crime of fashion."

Chapter 6

I know He's here, but I don't look near as often as I
should...His fingerprints are everywhere.

—"I Saw God Today" by George Strait

I'm often asked how I survived those early months.
One's first instinct—and certainly mine—when hit with
something traumatizing is to retreat, to pull away, to hide
and heal. Although tempting, it was not an option—and
maybe it never is. We are meant to live in community.

Right after Mark died, there was one place, and only
one place, I wanted to go: to church. To get there felt
crucial to me. I needed to be in that community and
worshipping God with that community. I also wanted to
model for the kids that we had nothing to be ashamed
of, and the proper place to turn was to God. So the kids
and I went to our church, Austin Ridge, the first Sunday
after Mark's funeral.

The pastor's sermon that morning focused on the

second mile of a three-mile race. He said it was the hardest mile. You begin your race with enthusiasm and with a sense of urgency, he explained, but it grows long and soon you can't see the starting line behind you or the finish line ahead. In the second mile, you don't know if you can make it, and you can feel very alone, even isolated.

The sermon was for me. His words pierced my heart. The pastor was talking directly to me; God was talking directly to me. Again He was saying, *I am here*. In that moment, I understood deep in my soul that just as everyone had eyes on me, God did more. I was not the first to run a hard race and I would not be the last—and I was never alone.

That morning, I was early in the first mile, but my lawyers had warned me we had years of litigation ahead of us; I faced possible bankruptcy; and a jail sentence was not off the table. I lived with the daily fear that the FBI could actually think I was involved. The second mile was coming. It would be long and hard...

And God would see us through.

I had already awakened early each day to spend time with God and had actively chosen to trust Him daily. It really did feel that deliberate. With all that was coming at me, it felt like I could lose my step at any moment, and give in to the panic and the unknown. Spending each morning in Scripture grounded me. Now I handed Him not only the daily journey, but all the emotions that assaulted me, too. I felt this surety that in the coming days my emotions were going to be shredded, were going to lie to me, and were going to make me feel lost, alone, and ashamed, but that wasn't reality. I needed right then, sitting at Austin Ridge, to choose not to believe them—and to trust in Him.

I added that resolution to my list of rules—to trust God at every moment, not only with my actions but also with my emotions. Four rules now governed my days. I got up and showered, put on my makeup, and breathed in and out, trusting God with each of those breaths— and the decisions made and the emotions felt within them. It sounds childishly simple, but sometimes it's all you can do as you take steps from the first mile into the second and even on to the third. You simply start stepping.

Choosing to trust didn't mean I wasn't swamped with questions. I couldn't keep them from spinning around my brain. My kids too were still asking them. Madison, especially, found my "I can't share that" answers very hard. It was hard for me, too. I carried so much alone and wrestled with so many questions—as well as with fear, anguish, and sorrow—and none of it I could fully share with anyone. I'd lost my best friend, my husband, and the father of my children. For the twenty-two years of our marriage, I had turned to Mark for everything. And now when I faced my toughest trial, he wasn't there to provide any guidance or answers. Not to mention that he was that trial's author. I also wasn't able to attend therapy because any and all discussions could be subpoenaed by the investigating agencies or by the court if litigation began.

That said, even then I knew the answers weren't mine to have. If Mark had been beside me and I'd been able to poke him in the chest and ask all my questions and pour out my anguish, he wouldn't have had the answers I needed. I suspect he wouldn't know them himself. Addiction and pain don't work like that, and Mark had been firmly in the grip of both for many years.

As I said, God made it very clear that Sunday morning that a race was ahead of me and that I needed to keep my eyes forward. I can't say I didn't look back now and then, but I definitely heard His directive not to dwell on the past. Looking back would only harm my children and me. Our present couldn't be found there, and certainly not our future.

One day a woman asked how I survived this time. I replied, "With a whole lot of F words." While I meant to offer a quick and witty retort, I soon realized the truth behind my statement. What I now call my "F words" got me through. I want to elaborate more about these F words: *Faith. Family. Friends. Fun. Forgive and forget.* I firmly believe they are vital to life. They remain five pillars of my life today. I need all five on good days, and I especially needed them—and continue to need them— on the bad. There are a few more I'll mention later— not pillars of my life, but inevitable words as one travels through life and tragedy.

FAITH

I started every morning with God in Mark's study. I've always been an early-morning person, but I got up even earlier those first few months. God was working daily in me and showing His gracious hand. Prior to Mark's death, I had been terrified to sleep in our house alone. When he went out of town, it wasn't unusual for me to call a friend and beg her to spend the night in our guest room. My friends laughed about it, but they also knew my fears were real, and one always came. Johnita, Bill Jones's wife, came to me right after Mark's death and offered for Bill to stay in our guest room anytime I needed him. I never took her up on that offer, nor did I ever call a friend. Since the night of Mark's death, I slept long and hard and without fear. Granted, I was shredded most days and beyond exhausted, but it was more than that. God took away my fears as clearly as He called me each morning to spend time with Him.

As I said earlier, I spent most mornings in the Psalms. They are so healing and encouraging. They cover the full gamut of human emotions and experiences, and express it all in prayers. Each prayer, whether it is filled with joy and hope, thanksgiving and praise, or pain and fear and contrition, became my prayer for that day. And often the Psalms mix emotions just like I felt them— anguish alongside trust, fear giving way to peace. Take Psalm 40 for example. Within it you find: *He lifted me out of the slimy pit, out of the mud and mire; he set*

my feet on a rock and gave me a firm place to stand (v.
2). A few verses later, you read how bad it is: *For my
troubles without number surround me; my sins have over-
taken me, and I cannot see. They are more than the hairs
of my head, and my heart fails within me* (v. 12). Then
a few lines later, you find a glorious moment of praise
and peace: *You are my help and my deliverer; you are my
God, do not delay* (v. 17). I rested in the understanding
and camaraderie the Psalms offered me, as well as their
hope and call to praise.

My dear friend Suzanne recently commented on
my daily prayers: "It was your food, your lifeblood
at that time, and I don't think you could've survived
without it."

She was right. Scripture started and ended each day
and filled moments in between. I could barely read and
certainly couldn't retain what I read, so I wrote down
on notecards short passages that spoke to me. Soon I
had a large bowl full of those cards, ready to be pulled
out at a moment's notice. And, even in the midst of fear
and pain, they brought me peace—God brought me
peace. That's what I tried to claim and trust every day
among the jarring emotions that always came layered
and multifaceted.

Two verses from Philippians also guided me from the
first moment I opened Mark's file in my closet: *And my
God will meet all your needs according to the riches of his
glory in Christ Jesus* (4:19). That verse had been posted
on my wall for years. It took on a new life for me while

everything else felt tumultuous. Philippians 4:12 also brought hope:

> *I know what it is to be in need, and I know what it is to have plenty. I have learned the secret of being content in any and every situation, whether well fed or hungry, whether living in plenty or in want.*

I did not know how things would end, and these verses offered the assurance that we would be cared for along the journey, no matter the outcome. We rarely have control over the outcome anyway, but we do have control over our actions and reactions along the way. Both these verses gave me the hope and the promise that as I became familiar with "any and every situation," no matter what it brought, we would be fine.

I've already shared with you 1 Timothy, but I'd like to elaborate on it here. Verse 6:10 states: *For the love of money is a root of all kinds of evil. Some people, eager for money, have wandered from the faith and pierced themselves with many griefs.* I clung to that verse not because it mentioned money and directly related to my circumstances, but because it mentioned a right order of love. It wasn't about the money. Money itself is a tool. It didn't get us into our mess—that would give it too much importance. The "love of money," however, played a large role. Money and all other "idols," be they popularity, influence, image, or status, had to be put back into a right relationship within my family.

And that's where another verse I've mentioned came in. *"Caesar's," they replied. Then he said to them, "So give back to Caesar what is Caesar's, and to God what is God's"* (Matthew 22:21).

That was my starting point. To return what was rightfully another's felt like the beginning of a new and right walk for my family. It wouldn't be easy; I understood that. Already it wasn't easy. But I hadn't been promised easy—none of us have. God never once said, "Believe in me and your life will be filled with buttercups and daisies, and no suffering whatsoever." He said just the opposite, in fact. Luke 9:23 makes Jesus's command pretty clear. *Then he said to them all: "Whoever wants to be my disciple must deny themselves and take up their cross daily and follow me."* First-century folks knew exactly the horrors of what "carrying a cross" meant. No matter what our suffering is, what our burden is, we are to bring it to God—that was also part of the "right relationship" I was chasing.

I only wanted one thing for my family...well, two. I wanted to make things right by everyone involved, and I wanted my kids to stick close to God. I didn't want any of this to turn their hearts from Him. I hoped my kids would see that whatever I did or was able to do was done with a heart that gave God glory, and that they would chase that. But I couldn't say it. Nothing I said at the time would have made a lasting impression; I needed to lead by example. They needed to see it in me. They also needed to understand that the outcome—of all of it—was in His hands, and we could accept that. That's where another verse from Philippians came in—I guess I was spending significant time there, too: *Do nothing out of selfish ambition or vain conceit. Rather, in humility value others above yourselves* (Philippians 2:3). So with that in mind, with as hard as everything felt and with the speed at which the tough revelations rolled me, I worked to do the right thing, and I relied on one truth to know what that "right thing" was: *Trust in the Lord with all your heart and lean not on your own understanding; in all your ways submit to him, and he will make your paths straight* (Proverbs 3: 5–6).

It was during this time that I realized how many times the word "heart" is mentioned in the Bible: 830 times. It is mentioned more than even "love" or "forgiveness." I had always collected hearts. They sit on tables, hang on walls, and are the decoration throughout my house. But God showed me so much more as He drew my heart to His with this word. Over and over, with each verse I read, I felt His peace. He said every morning, *I am here and I know your heart.*

FAMILY

Giving is my love language. Initially I found it hard to receive help and much harder to ask for it. I suppose I'm not alone in this. Needing humbles us. Needing makes us feel vulnerable, and that is never comfortable.

But I needed family to help with the daily business of running my life; I needed family to help in meeting the needs of my kids. I needed family to help me not to retreat and feel swallowed up by our struggles. Both sides of my family, and especially all my kids' cousins, were life-saving and life-giving to us at that time. Our house remained filled with family and friends that entire summer. And when kids weren't playing at our house, friends took my kids with them, whether it was to play mini golf, see a movie, or visit a local water park. Madison, Boone, and John Luke desperately needed that extra love and those extra graces—as did I.

We got hit so hard when Mark died, and we were still reeling at the end of the summer. A dear friend could not look at Madison without crying because her own father had committed suicide when she was Madison's young age. She taught me, by her tears alone, how long my kids would miss their dad and how much this would hurt for their entire lives. When discussing that time now, my kids still talk about the importance of that love and care. Boone commented, "I didn't want to think about everything. It hurt too much, and to have friends and my cousins around made me feel okay, that we'd all be okay." I will be forever grateful for my family, and friends who became family during those months.

But I had a role to play within my family as well, and I needed to remember that. My kids needed a parent.

One afternoon in June, twelve-year-old John Luke said some nasty things to a friend while standing in our kitchen. He wasn't saying or doing anything another twelve-year-old wouldn't have done—and that was the point. Had he been a normal twelve-year-old boy, I would have gently called him out on his behavior. So that's what I did. ·

"I know you're having a hard time, but that doesn't change our rules. We don't treat people like that."

John Luke stayed silent, so I sent him to his room to think things over. His friend ran off to play with others in our backyard.

A friend chided me. "You need to go easy on him right now. He's hurting."

"No." I blurted the word before I'd thought further. I then worked out my own approach as I articulated it. "Our rules still apply. I can't let this change how we live or who we are. He still has to do the right thing. He still has to be kind. We're not going to use this as an excuse to not behave the way we're supposed to." I then followed John Luke to his room to lay it out just between the two of us.

This isn't to say I got all my parenting right during those days or that my friend didn't have a legitimate opinion. After all, I had never been a single parent before, and she was right, John Luke was dealing with things that didn't affect most twelve-year-olds. But I hoped there was stability in rules and in right behavior, and I still believe I was right in that moment. That didn't make it easy. To try to impose "normal" in a situation that is anything but normal is always a difficult balance. And, although I was always the disciplinarian in our family, I had relied on Mark to provide strong backing. Without him, I felt alone and overwhelmed and questioned a lot of my decisions—the stakes felt so high. So, yes, I got some things right and others very wrong. I definitely snapped when I shouldn't have, showed impatience often, and was absent a lot.

But that's another beautiful aspect of family, too—extended family was there to love my children, and my kids forgave me my occasional outbursts and my absence. And as I said, Mary Beth was present all summer. My sister was such a blessing to my kids and me. Not only is Mary Beth the older sister I turn to when help is needed, but she is also a licensed grief counselor and social worker. She never pressed my kids to talk or share, but she was available when they did want to share, and for so many moments when they couldn't say anything at all. She gently guided them step-by-step through their confusion, grief, anger, and acceptance in ways I would not have been able to. And, although my parents and Mark's had returned to their homes, they continued their daily phone calls. Their unconditional love, prayers, and listening ears made all the difference.

In fact, my family and so many of our close friends made such an impact on my children that, when asked what she learned from those early days, Madison replied, "You show up. You don't need to do anything or bring anything; you just show up for a friend or a family in need."

Yet despite how much we loved the presence of family and friends, I found there were times when the four of us needed to be alone. We often found ourselves piled into my bed as if pulled by a magnet. Just the four of us curled together downloading the day or laughing at some antic of one of our large dogs. We also visited Mark's grave-side alone. It was a way to be near him. It might sound strange, but I had grown up going to my grandparents' graves on holidays, and my kids and I had visited their cousin Johnny's grave often as well. None of us found visiting Mark's grave odd; we found it consoling.

On Father's Day, a month after Mark's death, the four of us went to his grave to spread his beloved dog's— actually Boone's dog, Molly's—ashes over his grave. It was a moment like so many others that brought laughter and tears—and it was only for the four of us to share.

FRIENDS

I've told you already how my friends showed up. They were incredibly caring and generous as they took care of my entire family. But there is so much more to share...Weeks before Mark died, my good friend Melissa and her husband, Ben, came to Mark and me. I call them "good friends," but in many ways Melissa and Ben are more like younger siblings. Melissa is twenty years younger than I am, and I love and trust her as I do Mary Beth.

They came to us because Melissa had been questioning her work at Young Life at the University of Texas.
She no longer felt that working there was the proper fit,
and God had been laying something new on her heart,
but she wasn't sure what that was. She and Ben were
considering adoption, but still felt uncertain about it. I
grabbed my Bible and read James 1:27 to her: *Religion
that God our Father accepts as pure and faultless is this:
to look after orphans and widows in their distress and to
keep oneself from being polluted by the world.* I assured
her that orphans and widows were close to God's heart
and that He would show them the way.

Two days after Mark died, Melissa quit her job at
Young Life and came to me in tears. "It wasn't about
adoption. It was about you being my widow."

Melissa was the first to my house almost every morning and the last to leave. As friends took my kids here
and there to keep them busy, Melissa managed their
schedules and knew the larger picture that held every
day and every week together those first several months.
They relied on Ben's salary for income in those months
because Melissa sacrificially cared for us. I can never
thank her—both of them—enough. Her care was a
beautiful God-given gift, another way He truly said to
me, and I believe to Melissa, *I am here.*

But there are so many kinds of support and one no
better than another. As Madison said, "You show up,"
however you can. One group of friends brought me
uncommon laughter during that time. When I reached

the end of my rope, which felt dangerously frayed most days, I often found myself in a moment of fun with a friend, or I received a text, or a call with a crazy plan.

One day I sat with Jill, texting another good friend David Wise about some prank he'd just pulled. He wasn't answering our questions straight, so I shot off Liar Liar Pants on Fire with the pants-on-fire emoji. Jill and I laughed and waited for his reply. Nothing came. I checked my phone again. I had accidentally sent the Liar Liar Pants on Fire to my criminal attorney Johnny Sutton and not to David. I was still terrified of Johnny, and now I was mortified and humiliated. I immediately picked up the phone and called him to apologize.

"I haven't seen it. I don't know what you're talking about."

"Please delete it when you do, and I am so sorry."

I tried to laugh—it soon mixed with tears—and a text from Johnny arrived: You'd be surprised how often I need that phrase in my line of work.

Some days texts and witty banter weren't enough to lift my spirits. On June 15, a particularly low day, Chrissy Ray called with a plan. "I'm coming to pick you up in fifteen minutes. We have work to do." She soon pulled into my driveway and refused to tell me what was going on or listen to my complaints that I couldn't handle any more "work" that day.

"They're out of town." I tapped my window at Mark and Jill Adams's house as she parked.

"Exactly." Chrissy grinned.

Inside I found her husband, Corey, David and Christie Gonzales, and Krista and David Wise.

David Wise held a stack of photographs. "Let's get decorating."

For the next couple hours, we changed out all the Adamses' family pictures with cut-outs from magazines and pictures of ourselves printed off David's phone; we scoured their attic and decorated their house for every holiday at once, complete with a fully dressed and staged Halloween skeleton in their closet and a decorated Christmas tree in their living room; we rearranged their kitchen; and finally we took a "family photo" of all of us sitting on their bed laughing. We also blew up the forty-foot inflatable Frosty that we had been putting in each other's yards for months, in their front yard. It was an afternoon I never expected and desperately needed.

That kind of fun continued. On particularly low days, I learned to reach out. I learned to say I needed help, and someone always made time for me. Whether it was drinking tea and laughing around my kitchen table, "stealing" David Wise's car and going for a spin, or moving that monstrously large inflatable Frosty around yards, friends showed up. But it wasn't all about fun . . . Friends showed up in tender and tough ways, too.

The first week after Mark died, two friends brought me handkerchiefs; one was one of their grandmother's. Both held me while pressing them into my hands and said, "You'll need this." I did need those handkerchiefs. The tears didn't stop for weeks. But more than that,

I needed the love those handkerchiefs represented. I didn't get it then. But I do now, and I still carry one in my handbag at all times. They are delicate. They are hand-stitched. And they are the embodiment of sweet compassion and tender love.

Another friend showed me great love during that time as well—in the way of truth. I suspect oftentimes that's the hardest way to show love. She later told me she had thought about her words repeatedly before saying them and felt it was her first "God thing" moment when she got the courage to articulate them.

I say, "That's a God thing" often. It marks that moment, or that thought, or that coincidence that isn't a coincidence at all. It's God showing up. It's another way of Him saying, *I am here.*

I was tucked into the corner of the sofa in Mark's study having a really hard time. It was a low day, and I had just poured out to Kate all that was assaulting me. I remember saying "hate" a lot: "I hate this. I hate all of it. I hate where we are; I hate what's ahead. I hate being alone. I don't even throw the pillows off my bed anymore. I stack all nine on one side. It's sad, and cold, and hard sleeping alone, and I hate it."

Kate let me rant for a while; then she said in a quiet voice, "It's going to be okay. It's going to get better, and the pillows won't always be a problem. You're going to fall in love again."

I shook my head in a long, slow motion. "Impossible. I will never trust another man again. This is life now."

The best way to explain how deep this feeling ran is to tell you that I ordered a double headstone for Mark. I couldn't imagine ever being married again, so when it came time to order the headstone, I had my name engraved beside his. I fully expected that my life would play out for however many years I had left and then I would be buried, still a widow, alongside my husband. I truly believed there wouldn't be love—that kind of love—for me again, since such love begins with trust, and I couldn't fathom such an emotional leap in my future.

Kate stared at me. "You're wrong." She said the two words softly, but with force. She let them sit between us.

I shook my head again.

"No. You have so much love in you that you will trust again and you will love again. That has not been taken from you. Don't you believe that lie."

We didn't say much more. I didn't want to hear much more. But her words lived within me and despite wanting to deny them, they gave me hope.

FUN

I described some fun earlier, and friends were the authors of much of our fun during that time. But I'd like to touch upon the perspective of seeking and noticing, as well as appreciating, fun a little more. It sounds paradoxical, yet I discovered that when you are at the bottom, your perspective changes and you see humor, even fun, in so much that you never noted before. Situations that irritated or angered me were cast in a new light. Everything got flipped, which isn't always a bad thing.

My kids love to tell a story from January 2012. That's not quite true; they don't really *tell* the story; they act it out—which is much worse. We had an international trip coming up and I learned our recently acquired Global Entry didn't cover John Luke. At the time, Global Entry was new and offices were housed only in major airports. So on our way home from a vacation in Carmel, California, I scheduled an appointment for John Luke at the LAX office during our layover.

But our Monterey to Los Angeles flight got delayed, and we missed our appointment. That meant, rather than speed through the lines on our upcoming trip, we would have to wait in customs lines like everyone else. *The inconvenience!* I threw my large purse to the ground, and in a fantastic two-year-old-temper-tantrum fashion actually dragged my purse by its long strap across the floor of the Monterey airport whining about the delay, the missed appointment, and the trial of those future lines. I'm still embarrassed by my behavior that day and, other than my kids' recitation, there is nothing humorous about the story. In fact, I hated when they told it because, in many ways, I had believed that fairy-tale image we projected was real, and this story showed my flaws. It proved I wasn't perfect. Yet it was the first scene that appeared in my mind and heart on another occasion that also held no inherent humor...

Soon after Mark died, Kathy Smith accompanied me on one of my first true errands out into the world. After the grocery store, I pulled into our neighborhood gas station, TarryTown Shell, and started filling up my car. I felt warm, and the smell of gasoline overpowered me. I looked down. A tear in the hose was spraying gas all over me, soaking me from chest to toes. The manager ran out screaming and dragged me to the side of the station, where he proceeded to spray me with water. I immediately thought, *This is far worse than a long airport line*, and I started to laugh because there was nothing else to do. By this time, I'd become fully aware of our imperfections, but getting hosed down like a dirty dog brought it home in a tangible way. Getting mad was not going to get the gas off me just as getting mad in that airport didn't miraculously supply John Luke with Global Entry.

I'm not telling these stories side-by-side to say, "See how far I've come," but to share with you an insight I had one wet day. I also share it to illustrate how far one's perspective can change. Which is probably a very good thing, since many of the "fun" moments from that time are not classically funny—including the day when Mary Beth, Lisa, and I cleared Mark's books from his study after our house finally sold in January 2014.

Mark had a series of leather-bound financial-planning

books with titles such as *Financial Integrity* and *Ethical Family Wealth Management*. As we cleared the house, we laughed so hard over those titles. As we dropped each into the giveaway box, we read the title aloud and declared, "Guess he didn't read that one!" or "He sure never cracked the spine on this one!" Despite the seriousness of it all, those titles and reframing our mess for that moment still brings a smile to my face.

Another memory that continues to make me laugh occurred two months after Mark's death. My law team was assembled around a massive conference table discussing strategy. It was the first meeting in which I met everyone. There were eight of them and one of me, with Bill Jones—my legal equivalent of a safety blanket— absent that day. In the end, I'm pleased he wasn't there because he'd still be laughing now at what happened.

About halfway through a very long meeting, the conversation shifted. A few of the lawyers had talked with other attorneys regarding famous financial cases and the legal machinations involved, and they told us what they'd learned. Bernie Madoff's name and case came up in the discussion. My heart sank. I truly believe that was the first time I absorbed the extreme severity of my situation. The questions started spinning: *How can they put my name in the same sentence with Madoff? Are we going to become household names? How will my kids survive this?* It was more than I could bear. Tears streamed down my face. I tried to subtly blot them with my handkerchief. It didn't work. There was no heaving sigh, but the tears kept flowing in fast streams I could not mop up. I sat there in silence, trying to act professional, but unable to stop the rivers pouring down my cheeks.

Johnny Sutton, the one I had so recently called a "Liar Liar Pants on Fire," stopped the discussion and turned to me. In a beautiful way I'll never forget, he said, "Becky, God will see you through this. Don't lose hope or faith."

I didn't know where Johnny stood in his faith, nor my other lawyers except Bill and Monte. But the fact that Johnny would stop a meeting and direct such kind, faith-filled words to me was yet another clear and direct reminder from God: *I am here.*

Someone then suggested we take a break and, after thanking Johnny, I ran—thoroughly embarrassed—to the ladies' room. I berated myself the entire way: *Pull up your big-girl pants and get it together.*

Inside the bathroom stall, I realized I had completely forgotten my panties that day. I'd been so nervous, I'd changed my dress at least four times and had gotten so distracted that I forgot my panties completely. There were no "big-girl pants" to pull up. My tears turned to a sobby laugh.

God certainly has a sense of humor. Madoff's name didn't bother me again that afternoon. Instead, I spent the next several hours with my legs tightly crossed struggling to pay attention to *anything* the lawyers said.

FORGIVE AND FORGET

Some people find it shocking when I say this, but I didn't have trouble forgiving Mark, because I didn't bear him any anger. Yes, what he did was wrong and, yes, we were in danger—jail was a real possibility—but Mark was a good man who got lost. And he was a hurt man who dug himself deeper into pain. I could not muster any anger to pitch against his agony.

Instead I found myself struggling to forgive others when they behaved badly; forgive myself when I behaved badly; and remember that God had it all in His hands. Second Corinthians 10:5 became very important to me: *We demolish arguments and every pretension that sets itself up against the knowledge of God, and we take captive every thought to make it obedient to Christ.* So many times I needed to take my spiraling thoughts and fears, my frustrations, and my temper to God and forgive like I'd been forgiven. I needed to "take captive every thought to make it obedient to Christ." It was my only way forward. Without actively working to do that, I knew I'd spiral downward.

It wasn't always easy.

I had a hard time listening when a friend complained about the cost of her divorce. She was the one leaving the marriage, and her divorce wasn't being contested in any way; it simply cost money.

I had trouble forgiving someone who replied to Madison's Instagram post on the fifth anniversary of Mark's death (the kids were allowed back onto social media after two years) by writing, "Was he such a great Christian man stealing $30 million from innocent people? Please." Madison switched her account to private that afternoon.

I struggled to forgive myself for my impatience and my temper and my desire to resolve the entire financial situation in my way, in my time, and with my outcome. Daily I worked to take my thoughts "captive" and rest in Christ.

Forgiving and forgetting wasn't and isn't always easy. But I did find the way there—and I work to remember it—*love*. First Peter 4:8 tells us: *Above all, love each other deeply, because love covers over a multitude of sins.* It's true. I fully believe that if we love the way we are called to love, then "forgiving and forgetting" becomes easier. It becomes part of our disposition, in the very same way that if we get mad at each insult, we'll be more inclined to get mad at the next one.

I found that the more I focused on how I am to love, the less I focused on the things that didn't matter, worrying unnecessarily and judging wrongly. I also discovered that answers for the decisions I needed to make became more clear. After all, nothing is more daunting than the idea of standing before God and justifying my actions and decisions—imagining that moment clarified my thinking. Romans 12:19 supports this. It says, *Do not take revenge, my dear friends, but leave room for God's wrath, for it is written: "It is mine to avenge; I will repay," says the Lord.* Your struggles may not involve "revenge" and "wrath," but the verse applies to frustrations as well. It invites us to leave all stresses, wrongs, concerns, and fears in God's hands. As for love? He can supply that, too. After all, as George Strait, who opened this chapter, says in "Love Without End": "You see daddies don't just love their children every now and then, it's a love without end."

FRUSTRATION

This is linked with my thoughts about forgiveness, but there is more to say.

Surrender is a tough thing. Patience is not my strong suit. And this journey tested every fiber of my being. All valleys and tough roads test us. All suffering tests us. And we will face suffering. No one avoids it, but through it we can be refined. We constantly wonder, ask, and shout, *When will this end? Why can't I get out of this? If only... Why doesn't...* The permutations our frustration can take are endless—and I can only offer a friendly, "I'm right there with you."

I will say this, however: It astounds me how little truly is in our control. I never believed that before this journey started. If asked, I would have said I had a firm grasp on my kids, my marriage, my life, our finances, and our future. I'd give Mark credit for being the head of our family, but I would acknowledge I wielded a great deal of control in our home and for our future. None of that was true. I controlled nothing.

In the end, I believe the only control we can truly exercise is how we act and react in life, in times of grace, and good, and plenty, and in the desert and along the tough road. It sounds like so little, yet I've learned that is what we remember best, too. The outcomes aren't what necessarily haunt us or please us in the end, but how we handle the journey might. That's why the Global Entry temper tantrum and the wet-dog wash-down remain important to me to this day. They remind me that my behavior, and my heart, which guides my behavior, matter at every moment. They also remind me that whatever state I'm in—fairy tale or tragedy— God's in control, and there is always a silver lining on the horizon.

FEES

At this time, Fees was a big F word for me—which could sometimes lead to that four-letter F word we aren't sup-posed to say. I noted earlier and I'll allude to it more, but I was paying on average $100,000 to my attorneys each month. Prior to this I had no idea what a good attorney cost, much less eight of them. I was also initially paying those attorneys with money borrowed from my parents and from Mark's. That only compounded the burden of guilt I felt for needing so much, for taking so much.

We all have fees in our lives. They can be financial, emotional, physical...They can take any form. Yours may not look like mine or like your next-door neighbor's, but again I'm right there with you—we all have them. They are closely aligned with the previous F word, frustrations, and while they all look different, at their core they are the same. Our troubles evoke universal emotions. You may not have walked my road, but you might be able to understand my fear, loss, pain, panic, sadness, and worry—and I would bet, if we sat down over a cup of coffee and shared the stories, I'd understand yours.

Looking back at that time and these F words— positive and negative—one overarching reality comes to mind. We need grace. We need to accept it, give it, and live in it. Perhaps giving it to ourselves is the hardest part. It was for me. To accept that I was not perfect, that I was in a mess beyond my control and beyond anything I ever imagined for myself, and that I needed help in every way possible, was tough. But oddly, it came in a flash, and I had to catch up to the truth. As I grew in my faith, tested by this trial, 1 Corinthians 13:11 provided a loving road map: *When I was a child, I talked like a child, I thought like a child, I reasoned like a child. When I became a man, I put the ways of childhood behind me.* Accepting grace helped put those childish ways behind me.

Chapter 7

You're not supposed to say the word "cancer" in a song. And tellin' folks Jesus is the answer can rub 'em wrong...

—"This is Country Music" by Brad Paisley

As spring bled into summer, my mind repeatedly cast back to what I now call the "second mile" sermon. I found comfort in knowing many had survived "second miles," because I was so worn from the rush of May, and the end was nowhere in sight. This was my life now—I met with three of my primary lawyers, Bill Jones, Monte James, and Jerry Jones, most days and for a good part of the day. Sometime in June, Bill and Monte started scheduling the start of our meetings at lunchtime. They said it was for a change of scenery, but I suspect they both worried I wasn't eating. It was obvious I was losing too much weight, but everything was still going straight through me. Although I slept at night and felt peace within, I lived in a state of fight-or-flight tension and cried at the end of each day. I guess we aren't simple creatures. We can feel a lot at once, and I ran the emotional gamut daily.

I soon discovered another possible reason for the lunches. It's much easier to deliver bad news in whispered tones in public and over good food. Bill and Monte developed a good cop/bad cop routine, switching off who would "hit" me while I ate my burger and they enjoyed their salads—those men are such delicate eaters. Bill would only join me on the "dark side" when we ate at the Second Kitchen and Bar on Congress—then we'd both order the fried egg sandwich. There was plenty of bad news—so there were plenty of lunches. Bill quipped one day that he was surprised I stayed standing after "getting punched in the gut every day, week after week." According to him, I have "brass ovaries."

Each lunch was filled with disclosures and decisions. For one, we needed to formally decide how to handle communications with the three investigating government agencies, the SEC, FBI, and DOJ. Within weeks, Johnny Sutton recommended we follow a policy of full disclosure and cooperation, and I agreed. That doesn't mean that lawyers who don't decide on such a policy are hiding something; it simply meant we wanted to proactively show I was completely unaware of Mark's dealings and was committed to paying everyone back as soon as possible. Unlike Invesco in those early days, each agency took us at our word and treated me with kindness and respect rather than suspicion. They sent all their subpoenas, communications, and inquiries through my lawyers.

We also had to decide how to deal with the press. News outlets were still trying to get information and seeking comments. Most creditors didn't talk, and the stories were thin at best, but how long would that last? The show *American Greed* had contacted several creditors and appeared to be ramping up for an exposé. That especially worried me. Such a piece was going to be a prime-time feature. If no one talked, we hoped interest would fall away. We prayed creditors would feel the same and remain quiet, too.

Our daily discussions were also filled with creditor issues and the complexity of the financial situation. Who was calling my lawyers? Did what they claimed Mark owed them match with Mark's creditor list? We discussed which creditors I could not speak to at all, regardless of the conversation topic, and how the FBI might interpret any conversations. We addressed specific creditor situations, such as the collective that had formed, the creditor who held a lien on one of Mark's insurance policies, and the creditor who had already filed a claim against Atlantic Trust. We addressed protocol if I felt I was being followed, by the FBI or by creditors who had hired their own private investigators to track my movements. We discussed the paying of bills and which accounts could pay for what, as the estate was under dependent admnistration.

Jerry also filed papers with the court on a continual

basis, as every move I made needed court approval. Every time something came in, I deposited it into the estate's accounts. To me, every penny that came in meant a penny more for the creditors. It didn't feel like much—the proceeds from the sale of Mark's car, the returned money from Madison's canceled summer trip, the refunded membership fees from Mark's golf clubs, and even a five-dollar refund from AT&T—but it all mattered.

We also discussed the insurance money. That proved one of the toughest issues to address. First and foremost, we didn't know which if any of the policies would pay out, because we didn't have an official death certificate. The justice of the peace in Mason County had gone on vacation before submitting it. Without it, the insurance companies would not discuss Mark's policies. While all Mark's policies had dated out of the suicide exclusion clauses and were self-funding, there were other legal issues to consider. We simply did not know how much would, or even could, be available to creditors, and when.

Creditors grew anxious. In fact, a creditor later told me, "Seventy-five percent were sure you wouldn't pay."

Nevertheless, over each meeting and during each lunch, without the money in hand, we took steps toward the day we would receive it. We wanted the creditors—whose lawyers watched every step I made and every petition submitted to the court—to see I was sticking to my purpose and was working toward the best outcome.

Monte referenced it in his billing summary for May.

5/29/13: Meeting with Bill and Becky specifically we re-addressed the issue of giving away all of her assets including those that may be fully exempt from creditors. We discussed this issue at length on Monday, Memorial Day, and Becky was adamant that this was her decision. We called her into the office today so that we could address it personally as friends felt we should not do that. Becky said she appreciated their opinions very much; however, it was fully her decision and that she understood that there was some possibility of keeping some amount of the money, but she didn't feel right about keeping the money given the amounts taken by Mark, and she was fully cognizant and unemotional in her decision to let it go.

During this time, my lawyers did insist I keep one insurance policy. Although we did not know if Atlantic Trust would pay it out, my lawyers announced at the May 31 creditors' meeting that Mark had a $2.5 million insurance policy through his employer. They also announced that they were demanding I keep that policy because, as Bill noted, by working to pay everyone back, I was taking on all legal debts. While creditors could—and many did—hire their own attorneys, they didn't need to. I was trying to make the process as easy and fee-free for them as possible. All creditors in the room that day gave their support for me keeping those funds. I was the only one against the idea. But when faced with my financial reality, and my mounting legal bills, I acquiesced. I had to accept the policy because I had no way to pay bills, and I couldn't keep borrowing money from my parents and Mark's parents.

Another issue we discussed was debt. While we had pared back our expenses in every way possible, the house was a burden. It was too large and too expensive for my circumstances. We also discovered Mark had accrued more than $200,000 in credit card debt. Jerry Jones advised we negotiate a reduced payment. He quoted the standard rate as ten cents on the dollar.

I refused. "It's not right. We didn't spend ten cents on the dollar."

"It's not illegal. It's how these cases are handled . . . And we should talk about your mortgage. You need to stop paying it."

"I'm not defaulting on the mortgage, either," I said. I couldn't set that example for my kids.

"Again, it's how these—"

Jerry and I went round and round on these issues. His proposals were not wrong, but they were not right for me.

Bill chimed in occasionally. "She's going to do what she wants to do."

One recurring and important topic in early June was the impending FBI search of my home and my subsequent interview.

Johnny Sutton had been very serious with his warnings about not throwing anything away. "Not a paper, not an email. It will look like you're covering something up, and that is always worse."

I wanted to clear the house, though. I was anxious to list it for sale and get out. Not only was it too expensive, but it also felt dark and oppressive without Mark. It belonged to a family we no longer were, and it was just a house. Moving within it often reminded me of Kristian Bush's song "Trailer Hitch": "You can't take it with you when you go. Never seen a hearse with a trailer hitch."

Everything had changed for me. My view of *stuff* had changed; none of it mattered anymore. I had cleared into piles what I could, throwing nothing away, and I was ready for the next step. I had also stayed away from Mark's closet and his personal spaces, such as his bathroom cabinets and desk drawers. Again, Johnny didn't want me to see or learn anything new. It was important during my FBI interview that I be very clear on what I knew and when I learned it.

To fully understand what the FBI would find in my home and what questions they would ask about it, Johnny sent former FBI agent Matt Gravelle through my house first. He searched every drawer, cabinet, file, nook, and cranny. He copied our computer hard drives and searched them as well. He found a notebook in Mark's closet outlining several of our marital counseling sessions, which started a new round of questions to learn more about the "warts" in my life. After all, the FBI would also find that notebook and could press for answers, too.

After questioning me, Johnny requested I call my personal counselor and our marriage counselor to make a summary of their notes. I also needed to sign a release to give those summaries to my attorneys. Again, he didn't want any surprises. He needed to know the overall content and tenor of our sessions.

By that time, I really had no secrets from him, or from Bill and Monte. In fact, my lawyers not only knew my past, but they also knew my present better than anyone—and they protected me. When another of my attorneys went to our couples therapist for his summary, he was also handed a bill for making that summary. He was disappointed and told me later, "When I got the notes, I was handed a bill that I'm not giving to you because I know you'll pay it. With all you're going through, I can't believe he charged you for this little bit of work. If you get another, you can decide what to do with it."

I never received another bill, and I'll always remember all the compassion and concern he had for me—and that all of them did.

The FBI set June 13 as the date they would search our house. The night before, Christie, Jill, Melissa, and Lisa gathered around me as I sat on the kitchen counter. They laid their hands on me and we prayed. We prayed that the search would go well and that the media wouldn't find out about it. It was one thing to have my attorneys go through my house, but now agents from all three agencies, FBI, DOJ, and SEC, would search and remove anything and everything they deemed necessary for their investigations. While this massive search made me anxious, the prospect of them conducting it under the all-seeing eye of the media terrified me.

I told Madison and Boone about the search, and they joined Mary Beth and Lisa, along with John Luke, on a family outing. I simply couldn't tell John Luke. It was too much. I couldn't find any words to tell my twelve-year-old son that the FBI, DOJ, and SEC would scour our home looking for evidence of criminal activity. Friends kept him busy all day and, because they'd been doing it so often, he never suspected anything was amiss.

That morning, tensions were high in the house. In the late days of May, I had begun to compile an inventory for the court of everything we owned. Jerry Jones said I was allowed to keep $60,000 worth of goods within the home, but the court could requisition anything beyond that amount to pay the creditors. So not only could I not throw anything away, but it also I felt like I no longer owned much of it—or at least I needed to be able to let it go.

This destroyed my mom. Every aspect of this time was hard for her, but seeing how little I could keep or control was too much. As I wandered the house that morning, my mind cast back to her last visit, which had ended only days before.

I collect hearts, glass hearts, wooden hearts, porcelain hearts, any and every kind out there...and my favorite is a modern and scored crystal heart my mom and my nephew selected together before my nephew died in 1998. The day I was cataloging the living room, I noticed the heart was missing from the table.

"Mom, where's the heart you and Johnny gave me?"

She heard the steel in my voice. "Don't get mad. I took it. You have to keep it. They can't expect you to give up everything."

Staying out of jail and complying with all the rules I'd been given meant more to me than sentiment that morning. "You have to put it back. I could go to jail. Do you get that? These people aren't messing around. It has to be on this list and it has to remain here. I could go to jail!"

Without another word, my mom got her handbag, returned the heart, then hugged me.

Eventually I stopped yelling, stopped sobbing—and apologized.

Now that heart, along with all the others, sat on the living room table ready for the big day. I looked around the house one last time. It felt so foreign and even cold to me. Lisa, who was staying with me in the house, opened her laptop, as she'd been instructed to do, and left it on the counter to be searched. We all walked out.

We left the front door unlocked and, while Lisa joined Mary Beth and the kids, I spent the day at Kathy

Smith's house. She lived nearby, and I needed to be ready and available at any time to answer questions.

Late that morning, I received a frantic call from our yard guy. I had let his service go the week after Mark died, yet they still worked our yard as a gift to us. "My crew called me. There are vans and lots of people inside your house, Becky. There are people everywhere."

I had warned my neighbors, but I hadn't thought about the yard crew. I could only imagine the vans and the blue windbreakers with FBI written in yellow. "Will you just ask your guys to leave and don't tell anyone."

One call, and the news vans would return in a heartbeat.

The yard crew left and no one else showed up. No media witnessed twenty-six federal agents searching my house and carrying out boxes of papers and computers to their vans.

Once the agents left, I was a whirling dervish of activity. I started sorting through every square inch of that house, culling through twenty years of family life, determining what to throw away, what to sell (with court permission), and what to move with us to a future smaller home. We also petitioned the court and were granted permission to put the house on the market immediately.

One day, scouring through Mark's closet, I found an album of risqué pictures I had made for my husband early in our marriage. I felt heat flood my face, and I might have screamed. Not only could the agents have seen these pictures, but Johnny Sutton and Frank Bryan had possibly seen them as well.

I immediately called Bill, panicked. He burst out laughing. "That's hilarious. This is good...You have to ask him, but you can't until I'm around. I need to see his face so I can see his reaction. I'll be able to tell if he's lying."

I didn't get a chance to ask Johnny until months later. We happened to be alone after a meeting and were discussing other items found in Mark's closet and their possible implications.

"What about..." I stalled, then dove in. "Did you see any pictures I made for him? Something I had done just for my husband?"

"No." Johnny shook his head in confusion. "I didn't see a picture."

"Good." Relief flooded me. "I know you're telling the truth, because it wasn't *a* picture. It was a whole album."

Johnny's jaw dropped, and our meeting ended.

⸺

On July 12, my lawyers published the mandatory public notice:

NOTICE TO ALL PERSONS HAVING CLAIMS AGAINST THE ESTATE OF STAN-LEY MARK POWELL. *Notice is here-by given* *that original Letters of Dependent Administration for the Estate of STANLEY MARK POWELL were issued on the 25th day of June, 2013 in Cause No. C-1-PT-13-001037 pending in Probate Court No. One of Travis County, Texas to: REBECCA LEE POWELL. REBECCA LEE POWELL's mailing address is: Rebecca Lee Powell*

C/o Jerry Frank Jones

400 W. 15th St. Ste 975

Austin, TX 78701

All persons having claims against this Estate which is currently being administered are required to present them within the time and the manner prescribed by law. By: /s/ Jerry Frank Jones, Attorney

Creditors had been calling Monte, Bill, and Jerry since the first days after Mark's death, but now we entered the official procedure by which claims needed to be filed. This notice gave creditors thirty days to submit claims against Mark's estate. They started pouring in.

We had 120 days after a claim was submitted to either accept or reject it as legitimate. This didn't signal we had the money to pay it, just that we recognized its right to be paid. Our ability to make these determinations was complicated by the fact that Invesco's forensic accounting wasn't finished yet. It felt like we were chasing moving targets with a 120-day deadline to get it right.

Creditor tensions ramped up a bit more during this

process. We needed their records substantiating their claims; we needed to dig into Mark's records; and we needed to run everything by Invesco and confirm it with what their numbers said—all beneath the watchful eyes of all the creditors and the thirty-six lawyers representing them at that time.

Rumors had also gotten around that my lawyers were investigating clawbacks. A clawback is when you metaphorically put your hand over a pile of money that was paid as an excessive gain and "claw" it back to you. This meant that any creditor who had earned a large amount of interest on a loan to Mark could have those funds seized by the court. This prospect raised the pitch among the creditors to "mob" status. Many creditors had been Mark's friends, and they felt duped and betrayed, and now exposed. My lawyers and I spent many lunches debating the legality, feasibility, desirability, and necessity of clawing back all the interest gains made from Mark.

I was against them from the first. "I can't go to friends who made interest off Mark's loans and demand it back."

Jerry was equally firm. "It's a substantial amount of money. It's not optional. Invesco, the government, someone is going to insist on this because it can be used to repay the outstanding loans."

The whole idea turned my stomach. "I don't want it anyway. It's not about the money; it's about what's right and all that feels dirty." Again, I needed to be able to say to my kids and to myself that we paid for our lives; we paid for our memories. If we clawed back gains made years before from people, it felt like we were still using those people to settle our debts and to pay for our lives here and now. Emotionally, having that money available to pay the current loans felt just like asking for that money to pay for a trip or for a debutante ball. It felt wrong.

It was that sense of wrongness, concern, and even shame that made me push back on the clawbacks, and as I said, from going out in public. I didn't want to be seen and thought to be having a good time while all these rumors swirled around town. However, one evening during this time, Mary Beth persuaded me to go to a friend's house for dinner. Although it was going to be only the Armstrongs, Eddie Safady, Mary Beth, and me, I still resisted. After all, I'd only gone to lunch with my lawyers, the grocery store, and the gas station by that time. But this was for a close friend, at her home, and I agreed. I arrived a few minutes late with a bottle of wine in hand.

Eddie Safady, who always sent encouraging texts when there was an article in the paper, strode toward me and grabbed the wine.

He smiled and lifted the bottle. "Do we need to drink this fast? Is it Clawback Wine and they'll take it from us?"

I burst out laughing. I was so thankful not to evade the truth, but to face it from a different perspective.

The "second mile" was long, but in many ways summer flew by, too. I was in meetings every day, and the kids stayed close. Each evening I would come home and we'd spend time together. Friends had organized meals through August, which was such a blessing because, even though I love to cook, I was too tired to cook anything that summer. Melissa was at the house every day, handing all the details I couldn't, even helping to plan a few trips for the kids—the Fourth of July with Mark's parents in Colorado Springs and a few weekends with my family in Houston.

For my part, the meetings and the investigations pressed on. On July 29, the SEC subpoenaed Invesco and me for Mark's personal records and files, including the contents of his briefcase. It continued its investigation, as did the DOJ and the FBI. Invesco continued with its forensic accounting. My lawyers dealt with so much—including a search for the justice of the peace from Mason County.

She had gone on vacation prior to issuing Mark's official death certificate, but now, weeks later, it appeared she was AWOL in Alaska. Her office said she had gone fishing, but no one could reach her. No one had a date for her return. She had left her job in May and had not been heard from since. By August, my lawyers wondered if she had been killed in Alaska, since no one in her office knew anything, nor had they heard from her in weeks. Yet she was the only one who could issue an official death certificate. Without it, we could not get the insurance money to pay back the creditors.

We put out some inquiries and we waited, focusing our attention on other fronts, fronts that felt endless and exhausting. Claims kept pouring in; there were constant requests for reports; tax questions emerged; clawbacks were still hotly debated; and communications with Invesco remained ongoing and stressful.

When the kids were gone to either Colorado Springs or Houston, I found myself alone in the evenings as I had never been before. I met Mark when I was twenty-one and had been with him since that first date. I'd been married to him for over half my life and, although my friends were present and wonderful, I felt very alone. I wasn't kidding when I told Kate that I stacked all the pillows I'd once thrown to the floor on Mark's side of the bed. Doing that made my bed smaller, warmer, more...like what I'd known, and I didn't feel so small and alone. Each night when I pushed them aside I was reminded of Jonny Diaz's song "Thank God I Got Her." He sings of his love for his wife and her "nine fancy pillows on our bed." Mark had teased me about my pillows, too.

The evenings felt dark and sad, and often hard. Again, I cannot emphasize enough the consoling power of good country music. Sometimes songs make you laugh, sometimes they make you cry, and other times they meet you right where you are. Darryl Worley has a song, "Sounds Like Life to Me," in which a man complains to a friend about all the things hitting him that night: His wife is expecting, his washer quit, he's got bills to pay and little work with which to pay them...His complaints continue until his friend replies in a wonderfully melodic way that doesn't quite translate here: "Sounds like life to me, it ain't no fantasy. It's a common case of everyday reality." This song and so many others helped me not feel so alone.

Rascal Flatts also has a song that I leaned on heavily during that time. "Stand" tells listeners to get back up when they're so weighed down they can only drop to their knees. And after that, they're strong enough to stand again. I needed these words, and assurances that I would get back up again during those dark second-mile evenings.

I also learned an important lesson as the chaos of the early days steadied into a rhythm. Right away, I had focused on people judging our hearts. I had told my kids, "People are watching how we handle this." And I was right; we constantly drew stares and discreet pointed fingers in the grocery store. Now I learned I needed to extend that grace to others. I could not judge their hearts.

Near the end of August, I finally agreed to go out to dinner. My friends decided my inaugural dinner should be at our favorite restaurant, Uchi. Our group's texts started flying that morning. I was in meetings with my lawyers when the text thread began. I don't remember how the thread started, but I remember how it ended.

Chrissy Ray texted: Corey is still out of town. I don't feel like going out to dinner without him.

The conversation died. I later learned a separate thread started that sounded like this:

Are you serious? Did you really just text that to Becky?

How could you say that?

What???????

After my meeting ended, I read Chrissy's final text and replied: Really? Like I feel like going out to dinner without Mark? Get your ass there.

I was laughing, but Chrissy, already chastised by the group, texted back instantly: I'm sorry. I'm so sorry I said that. It's just that I have so much on my plate right now.

I shot back: Really? You have a lot on YOUR PLATE?

Of course I received another volley of apologies—which only made me laugh harder. Chrissy came to dinner and, for the first half, we had a wonderful time. I didn't forget all that surrounded me, but for brief moments it didn't overwhelm me. I didn't drink, but I laughed and ate…until I felt it.

Someone was watching me. Instinctively we know when someone is staring at us. I felt it in the grocery store. I felt it at the small deli where my lawyers took me to lunch. I felt it right there in Uchi. I looked up and clashed eyes with a woman across the restaurant. I recognized her immediately, and I glanced away. I felt humiliated, judged, and physically ill. My stomach bottomed out, and I didn't taste another bite. I ended the evening in my bubble bath, crying and listening to country music—though it was probably Carrie Under-wood's "Jesus, Take the Wheel" that night rather than "Stand."

My first night out had been a mistake, and I began to believe I would never escape the weight of this scrutiny and condemnation.

Two days later a letter arrived from the woman. My hands shook as I opened the envelope... *I was so happy to see you out the other night. You and your sweet children are in my prayers.*

God whispered again: *I am here.*

And I cried again.

Chapter 8

Never compromise what's right and uphold our family
name. You've got to stand for something or you'll fall
for anything.

—"You've Got to Stand for Something" by Aaron Tippin

Although the heat doesn't abate in Austin until well into
October, summer came to an end on August 22, 2013.
That day Madison returned to Baylor University to start
her junior year and Boone joined her as a freshman.
An entourage accompanied them to Waco. Friends who
had cared for us all summer took time off work to send
the kids back to school in style and with love. Mark's
parents and sister joined us from Dallas; Jeff Stedman
flew in from Colorado Springs; my brother Johnny and
his son came from Houston; Melissa and Ben drove
with us from Austin; and Mark and Jill Adams, with two
of their kids, followed our cars.

The day was wonderful, but Madison and Boone
soon found themselves struggling. They were both in

their mandatory semester of once-a-week chapels that fall. One chapel during September, National Suicide Prevention Awareness Month, addressed suicide. When the presenter announced that suicide was the most preventable death, both my kids got up. Overwhelmed, they left the presentation—and both were reported for leaving chapel.

I was devastated to hear the news and sickened by how vulnerable my kids were each and every moment. After that initial rocky beginning, however, Boone found relief in the routine, in the focus on his studies, and in his anonymity. No one knew his story and our present struggles. He excelled in his classes and made the dean's list that first semester. Madison was not so fortunate. She was the recipient of some gossip and unkind words during the first weeks of classes. Although it died down fairly quickly, my heart still hurt for them.

Madison also had another setback within those first few days that rocked me to my core. In April 2012, while taking pictures for the Women's Symphony Debutante Ball, Madison had passed out, fallen backward, and cracked open her skull in two places. The injury had been so severe she was placed on anti-seizure medication and had lost all sense of taste and smell for a year. Madison had gone off her anti-seizure medication the month before Mark died in preparation for her summer semester in Italy, and had been well all summer. But on August 25, three days after returning to campus, I got the call that she'd had another seizure.

I grabbed John Luke and drove straight to Waco to get Madison to the hospital. We didn't pack bags, and I drove well beyond the speed limit. John Luke was terrified with my driving, but I was terrified I would have to bury my daughter. That is the level on which I was operating. At Waco, I picked up Madison, and forced Boone to join us, and I drove, pedal to the metal, on to Dallas and the hospital. I needed all of us to be together when the worst happened.

Madison was put on seizure medicine again for six months—and has been fine ever since. Mark's dad gave Boone a ride back to Waco. John Luke stayed with me another day before we could return Madison to campus then head home ourselves.

Later a counselor assured me my reaction was natural and expected: "Your imagination gets to that worst-case scenario much faster now because you know what it can actually look like." But my kids thought I had gone crazy and, to be honest, my instant hysteria and my certainty of doom terrified me. I couldn't think; I could barely breathe, and I was so sure I would lose my daughter. I couldn't envision another end to the incident.

Many friends have confirmed the therapist's statement and shared similar stories with me since that day. Once hit hard, our imaginations can take us right back to that visceral pain and panic. I had to work hard that day with Madison and continue to work to *take captive every thought to make it obedient to Christ* (2 Corinthians 10:5). Those aren't just words for me anymore. I know

now that my thoughts, ideas, and emotions can do as much harm as they can do good if I don't make them obedient to the love, mercy, and truth within Christ. I simply can't live my life in the state of panic I can dream up on my own.

But to do that isn't easy now, and it was especially challenging back then. Just as the kids settled into Baylor, I learned the *American Greed* show was gaining traction. Friends reported to me that a variety of shows and media outlets continued to contact them. I even received news that a full-spread *Texas Monthly* article had been written. The reporter reached out to Jerry Jones and me for an interview.

I became so nervous that I called Baylor to warn them that a television crew or reporters might show up on campus searching for Boone or Madison. I also asked friends to direct all queries to my lawyers and to please not answer even the most innocent of questions. I prepared my kids as best I could.

No in-depth television show was ever made, and no *Texas Monthly* story ever ran. We expected to find the article in each issue and were surprised, and thankful, when we didn't. While Mark's death and our present struggle was definitely headline news, no one talked to the press, which kept it from the public's eye. It was beyond extraordinary how little people shared.

One day, I feared my allotment of grace had run out.

John Luke called from school, frantic. He'd lost a composition notebook that was due in class and he suspected he'd accidentally thrown it away. I went out to the recycling bins in the carport. While I was out there, the dogs started going crazy. I looked up to see a stranger slowly walking down our quiet cul-de-sac, with a large camera. I walked inside, a little scared, and tucked my pistol in the back of my pants. Yes, I'm a true Texan with a pistol and a license to carry a concealed weapon. But, no, it's not usually in my pants.

I walked back outside as she paused in front of our house. I approached her, arms outstretched. "Please, could you not take any pictures?"

She coolly replied, "I'm from the *Wall Street Journal* and this is a public street. It's legal for me to take pictures. If you don't want to be in the picture, I'll give you time to go inside."

I turned around so as not to be in any of the pictures and heard a camera click. Immediately I remembered the pistol. I dashed into the house to call Johnny Sutton, certain I would be in trouble on some level. This would not look good.

Johnny had a policy. If I called him and he was busy, he wouldn't answer. If I called a second time, it signaled an emergency, and he would answer without fail. I called twice.

I blurted out the story in a complete panic.

"If they print a picture let's hope it's you and the pistol. That is a much better story than you digging around in your trash."

That was all he said about it. My grace hadn't run

out. The September 27, 2013, *Wall Street Journal* article featured a nice photo of Mark and a lovely photo of the house, but nothing of me, my recycling bins, or my pistol. Nor did the article mention my kids at all.

There were definitely some light moments too as fall darkened the skies earlier each night. I count the "pistol picture" as one of them now. Another was a lovely and encouraging call to Jerry Jones. Linda McCaul, Congressman Michael McCaul's wife, said that her husband was returning $25,000 to Mark's estate from past contributions that we had made to Congressman McCaul's campaign. She also said she hoped it would encourage others to do the same, and that she was so sorry for all we were going through.

Jerry, a staunch Democrat, was hilarious about the call. He quipped, "It gives me a little hope in the Republican Party."

But Linda's kindness meant much more to me. It bolstered me especially because many of our friends in the political arena seemed to disappear upon Mark's death.

My lawyers had warned me from day one that this journey could take years, but I hadn't believed them. In my mind it was simple: I wanted to pay everyone back, and everyone wanted to get paid back. I would, hopefully, soon have the money to do it, and all would be well and done. There were so many aspects of my life I wanted to reclaim or grow anew—and none of that could happen until everyone who was owed money got paid.

But nothing was moving as smoothly or as quickly as I desired, and I was running out of money. The court controlled everything but my personal checking account and, since Mark's death, no funds had been added to it. No paychecks. No deposits. And every penny that had come through refunds, returns, or items sold had gone into the court-controlled estate accounts. The kids felt my anxiety. Madison even now recalls John Luke getting upset with her when she wanted to buy a new toothbrush. Toothbrushes aside, there was still the mortgage to pay, the water bill, the grocery bill...Our money was almost gone.

I needed a job. I brought this up with my lawyers and was immediately set straight.

"You can't. Not yet. You're not out of this, Becky. We need you every day."

There was no stepping off this road, not even for a paycheck. I was so blessed to be able to ask family for help, but that still meant I was taking what belonged to others. I found our vulnerability and need hard to accept.

Along those lines, I had been telling the kids that we could keep what was special, but other stuff was going to be sold to repay the loans. They didn't know Jerry's allotted $60,000 number, but they knew in general what I faced. We talked as openly about it as we could and, as much as my perspective about money was changing, so was theirs.

One afternoon, I went up to check on John Luke in his bedroom and found him making piles.

"What are you doing?"

"I'm making a pile of stuff for you to sell because I know you need the money to pay everybody back."

I glanced to the pile as he pointed to his prize jerseys on the wall, a game jersey signed by University of Texas quarterback Colt McCoy and another signed by NFL quarterback Robert Griffin III. "You should sell those, Mom. They could be worth a lot."

John Luke simultaneously broke and lifted my heart. I don't even remember what I said to him. I just remember I went back downstairs and cried.

Within a few weeks of this conversation, Atlantic Trust paid out the $2.5 million retirement insurance policy that Bill had mentioned at the May 31 creditors' meeting. I immediately used the money to repay my parents and my in-laws for the retainer fees they generously paid for me in May and brought my legal fees up to date, more than $242,000 by that time. On that note, $2.5 million is a lot of money. It will always be a lot of money. But to put my financial situation and my attorney fees into perspective: By the time all was said and done, my legal fees alone exceeded $1.7 million.

Mason County's justice of the peace also returned from vacation and issued Mark's official death certificate in August. Usually it takes days to acquire a death certificate; Mark's took more than four months. It was an absolutely unbelievable delay, but one, once I was able to contain my impatience, I saw God's hand guiding. If the money had come in immediately, creditors and their lawyers would have been more eager to sue the estate to stake their claims. The turmoil and the waiting allowed tempers to cool—and the unique nature of this "hold" stunned everyone. It left everyone just off balance enough that no one started the cascade of lawsuits.

With the death certificate filed, the insurance policies paid out. My lawyers were stunned. I had expected all of them to pay—after all, Mark had paid the premiums. But I learned it wasn't so simple, and the fact that all did pay out, and so quickly once in receipt of the official death certificate, was another miracle.

Right before the funds arrived, Eddie Safady appeared before the court to describe his safety measures and logistics for keeping the money for the creditors. Soon $10 million was deposited into a sweep fund within Eddie's Prosperity Bank. The court also appointed a third-party trustee for the money. This trustee, also a lawyer, provided a further level of assurance to the creditors, as I now had no legal claim over the money at all.

The final $5 million life insurance policy paid out and was deposited into a separate account controlled by the court. Mark had used that policy as collateral for a loan, and the creditor refused to release his claim until he was assured no one else would come after him, for either payment or clawbacks, or come after me. He said he wanted the financial protection both for him and for us. He wanted to make sure the kids and I were going to be okay.

I mention this because it created a challenge and resulted in more than $20,000 in legal expenses alone. We had to be very careful to keep this situation calm and clear so that it didn't make other creditors feel unsure or less protected. Everyone was watching everyone else, and this move brought the whole tower into a precarious lean.

The day the funds hit the accounts, I asked the question again, "When can we pay everyone back?"

The tax attorney was silent for a beat on the call before answering, "Not yet. There is still the IRS. We need to file and wait for a ruling."

"How long does that take?"

"Once we file, they have eighteen months to review it."

While this was devastating news, I asked him to file immediately and counted the days, believing I could pay everyone back in March 2015.

There was plenty to do in the meantime... Invesco's forensic accountants issued their final report. They had tracked every cent, and we now knew exactly who, what, and when with regard to all Mark's financial dealings. The initial estimate of $38 million was finalized at $21.5 million. Invesco immediately paid $5.1 million to make Atlantic Trust's clients whole, then filed a $5.1 million claim against me.

This meant, Invesco's claim aside, I needed $16.4

million to repay every creditor 100 percent of their prin-
cipal money. Although it was an extraordinary number,
I was pleased to finally have a number and some clarity.
Yet with that clarity also came the mistakes we had
made. Without firm and final numbers, we had denied
legitimate claims because they didn't reconcile with
Mark's records.

"If we owe them money, we have to pay them," I said
at yet another lunch.

"They're not on Mark's list." Jerry shook his head.

"If they're on the forensic accounting list, we have
to pay."

Jerry explained that these men could not file a second
claim. If they wanted to be repaid, they would need
to file a lawsuit. While that was the next legal step,
it also raised concerns. First, a lawsuit was public and
could be potentially embarrassing for the men. Second,
it could incite panic in the other creditors. Lawsuits
were what we'd been trying to avoid—one spark could
start a flame.

I nodded to Jerry. "Then it's a lawsuit. You have to
make them file."

Jerry sighed and contacted each man individually. He
even drove to Houston to make an emotional appeal
to the final holdout. Jerry reiterated to each how much
I needed to pay them. In the end, all agreed and
filed suit.

Bill sent an email to all the creditors to warn them
of Jerry's actions and the impending suits. We wanted

to be perfectly clear what we were doing and why. He outlined that these men were not jumping the gun; they had been denied a rightful claim. Everyone seemed calm and understanding and patient.

Other issues also arose as final numbers became public. One creditor served me papers at home rather than serve the suit to Jerry's office, as every other creditor had done and as the lawyer had been specifically instructed to do. You see it in the movies all the time—people getting served lawsuits at home. But, I'll tell you, it felt horrible to receive such a motion. Jerry was furious with this situation.

In a second situation, a creditor continued to reach for an amount beyond Invesco's number. Jerry was frustrated because, as he told that creditor's lawyer, everyone's numbers had been calculated in the same manner. Yet the creditor had made two loans from two separate entities. We had combined the two entities and the two loans. The older loan had made a profit so we subtracted what the estate owed him against those profits and calculated his repayment to be $25,000. However, he wanted the accounts and the loans to remain separate, and his position had legal precedent. In the end, the lawyers determined the entities and the loans remained separate and, because we did not pursue clawbacks, his final repayment became a firm $292,500.

After weeks of negotiations following this, Jerry came to a meeting one day elated. "I've talked him down to $275,000."

I pounded my fist on the table. "No way. If the final accounting says we owe $292,500, that's what we're going to pay him. I'm never going to let anyone say I didn't pay back everything. I will never let him hold that over me."

Jerry stared at me, unable to comprehend my thinking. He then looked to Bill for support.

Bill shook his head and laughed. "She's going to do what she wants to do."

With a shrug, Jerry recorded the number as $292,500. I felt terrible. While I was certain about the number, I was sorry about Jerry's time and the effort he'd spent working the creditor down to $275,000—because that's what Jerry did; he worked to protect me at every turn. I came to adore that man for his protection of me, even when I wouldn't listen to him.

I needed to repay every penny. I truly felt that is what God wanted from me, and not to accept an easier way out on any level or in any context. While considering both these situations, Genesis 14:23 came to mind: *"That I will accept nothing belonging to you, not even a thread or the strap of a sandal, so that you will never be able to say, 'I made Abram rich.'"* It was important that I could only point to God for resolution to this matter. It was also important that my kids never feel that we had benefited wrongly from another or for someone to say that we hadn't done our utmost by them.

All during these legal and financial skirmishes, I cleaned out the house. It was on the market, and every day there wasn't a showing, friends and I culled each room, sorting it into giveaway, throwaway, or move-away piles and boxes. One afternoon, feeling at the end of yet another rope, I tackled the storage closet and found both Mark's and my childhood boxes. Within the one marked *Mark Powell Childhood*, I found Mark's "Decoupage Jesus." I call it that, but it's best known as one of the Sunday school art projects from fifty years ago. The kids picked out a picture of Jesus and Mod Podged it, if that can be a verb, to a wood board. They then took it home to Mom and Dad.

Mark's Decoupage Jesus was lovely—a picture of a placid, peaceful Jesus with eyes gazing to His Father above, glued to a wood board with a thick coating of Mod Podge. The edges had yellowed, but it still exuded peace, serenity, and confidence in the Father's love. I laid it aside and moved on to more boxes. Not two boxes later, in my box of childhood things, I found my own Decoupage Jesus. First, it's amazing that Mark had saved his, but that I had saved mine too is beyond remarkable. But that's not what dropped me to the floor in tears.

As a young child, I had not chosen a serene picture of Jesus with children, a placid Jesus looking to heaven, or a Good Shepherd Jesus gathering his flocks. For my Sunday school project, I had glued onto my thin wood board a livid Jesus in the midst of throwing over the moneychangers' tables inside the temple gates. His stern face was full of grim determination; His arms heaved the tables up and over, coins flying through the air. The passage, often described as the Cleansing of the Temple, can be found in all four gospels, and its image can be found on my Mod Podge board.

I sat on the floor sobbing. *I am here*, God said again.

Not only that…God added a little more that afternoon. *I have prepared you for this moment since you were a little girl.*

Once I stopped crying, I picked myself up and secured my small board to my bathroom mirror.

It still hangs there today.

Chapter 9

There ain't nothing that can't be done by me and God.
Ain't nobody come in between me and God.

—"Me and God" by Josh Turner

Soon after Madison and Boone's experience in the campus chapel, John Luke called home. His school had scheduled an assembly for Suicide Prevention Awareness Month as well.

He hadn't been able to leave and called distraught afterward. "There was an assembly on suicide today," was all he could say, and all he needed to say.

I drove to the middle school immediately to pick him up. I called Boone and Madison at Baylor, and the four of us had a sit-down conversation again as soon as we could to talk about suicide so that they could share how they were feeling. It was so important to me that we talk, again and again, until we almost felt there was nothing left to say. Yet we always found there was more.

It became clear to me, during this time, how pervasive suicide is and how vulnerable are those close to it. While I didn't want my kids to feel shame regarding Mark's death, there was no keeping them from the vulnerability of its nearness. I had to face it myself.

One afternoon in late October, after John Luke and I had moved out of our house, we walked our new neighborhood. A woman approached us, one of our new neighbors, to say hello. I told her my kids and I had just moved in down the street.

She immediately asked, "Where is your husband?"

"He passed away," I replied.

"Oh...I'm sorry. Cancer?"

"No."

"Well...how did he die?"

"He took his own life."

The questions ended there, but that wasn't the first time I'd gotten to that point that fall. Being a widow at forty-seven was unusual and always invited questions. And I answered them, promising myself never to shy away from the truth. But this was the first time John Luke had witnessed such a moment. He turned to me as we walked away. "Really, Mom? Why would someone ask that?"

"It's strange, but they do."

Although it was painful, it was a good moment for us. John Luke realized that I too faced the same questions he did and felt that same vulnerability every day. And it was vulnerability, for every time someone asked and I answered, I felt like I was inviting them into something hidden and private within our world—and they, for the most part, were strangers.

By this time, it really was *every day* that I felt like that, too. With fall, life resumes a more regular cadence, with routines around work, kids, family life, and more structured two-day weekends. With the kids back in school, I soon fell into those routines as well. While I was in meetings almost every day with my lawyers, those meetings no longer took the entire day. I started to run errands on my own and found there was a sense of normalcy and comfort in going to the grocery store or Office Depot. I still noticed people stopping, pausing, and glancing at me, but I was becoming more accustomed to it.

One day I was in Office Depot and ran into Karl Rove, George W. Bush's deputy chief of staff. He reminded me that in his book *Courage and Consequences*, he wrote of his mother's suicide.

Polly Crowell, whose husband, Brian, had talked to Boone about his own father the night Mark died, cried often about my kids. It brought up so many memories about how her father too had committed suicide when she was exactly Madison's age.

Over and over, especially as I stepped out into the world, I was reminded how pervasive and real suicide is. And, until it touched me directly, I didn't understand the "differentness" of it—the unique questioning pain it left behind. The hushed culture around suicide is changing and has gotten a little better, but it's still a hard road. As best I am able, I want to peel the curtain back on all we experienced during that time.

Suicide wasn't and isn't shameful. It's desperately, tragically sad. We were, and remain, deeply saddened by the way Mark died. But we were far more saddened by the pain that drove him to that point, a pain we weren't even aware of. Talking, sharing, and listening helped my kids and me handle our tragic loss far better than if we'd stayed silent and kept it bottled up.

Thankfully, there were humorous moments too around this serious subject. My sister Mary Beth called me, frantic, one afternoon. During John Luke's summer visits to Houston, she'd gotten him hooked on *General Hospital*. John Luke now recorded the show daily and called my sister to discuss the happenings.

"Has John Luke seen today's episode?" she asked. When I said he hadn't, she sighed with relief. "You need to delete it. A character committed suicide today. Delete the recording."

I did. Not only did John Luke not see that episode, but by missing a day, he broke his cycle of daytime drama. It was a win-win.

While both John Luke and I enjoyed the security of fall's routines, we also found ourselves somewhere we'd never expected—very aware of our aloneness.

Soon after Mark died, one of our Newfoundlands, Maxwell, died as well. He was eleven and getting old. It was expected, but it was beyond hard. My kids had grown up with Maxwell; he was the first puppy John Luke had ever known. There is no doubt Maxwell's loss hit us even harder because we were already grieving. Soon after that, Griffin, our other Newfoundland, left us, too, for a new home. He became depressed after Maxwell's death and was clearly upset and agitated with all the changes in the house and people constantly coming and going. I suspect Mark's absence also undid him, because Mark really did love the dogs best—or at least gave them the most treats. I also wondered, considering that dogs can smell a million times better than we can, if Griffin could smell the sadness in our home. Regardless, Griffin was not doing well: He refused to eat, and he was clearly stressed. We knew we needed to help him. So we gave him to a quieter family with time to lovingly care for him.

This left an even bigger gap in our home and our lives that fall. Until Maxwell and Griffin were gone, I hadn't noticed how comforting our dogs' presence was and how often we both talked to them.

Without Mark and the dogs, and with Madison and Boone away at school, each quiet evening at home felt heavy and somber. With only the two of us to participate, none of our routines or traditions felt right. So we began a new one that fall: *Monday Night Football*. I have to say, I am not a sports girl; I don't even like TV. But John Luke and I needed something for us. So every Monday night, he taught me the game of football. And while I still don't draft a fantasy league and I can't sit down and swap NFL stats with you, I can now throw out a few terms and cheer in all the right places.

We did not, however, get another dog right away. Though there was one funny moment where I almost said yes to my son.

A teacher at John Luke's school was giving away her mother's dog. Her mother had picked up the stray from a local park. One afternoon, she brought it to the school to let the kids and their parents meet it in hope that someone would adopt it.

John Luke called and asked if I would pick him up and come meet the dog.

Lisa was staying with me at the time. "Don't you dare get him that dog," Lisa said. "You know nothing about it. I had a shelter dog once and we couldn't calm her down. We had no idea what she'd been through, and she was snappy at times. John Luke is a kid. You can't do that."

I agreed with her. I also knew we were moving soon and to bring any dog into that chaos wasn't fair. While I was willing to meet the dog out of respect for John Luke's wishes, I had no intention of taking the dog home.

We arrived at the school and met John Luke in the side field where kids were playing with the dog. It was fuzzy and adorable, and John Luke's face was flushed with excitement, his eyes tear-filled.

"Isn't he great, Mom? Can we get him?"

I steadied myself for the gentle letdown when Lisa grabbed my arm. "Just get him the dog! How can you not? Can't you see how wonderful it is and how happy he his?"

My jaw dropped. Lisa heard her own words, and we both laughed in disbelief.

That's how life constantly felt. It could twist and turn at any moment. I wanted to make so many things—on any and all levels—right and safe and comfortable for my kids. But we didn't get the dog that day, and John Luke handled his disappointment well. After our experience with Griffin, he too saw the danger of upsetting a dog in our current situation.

Just a year later, an adorably hyper German short-hair pointer puppy named Birdie entered our home and erased all memory of that day from John Luke's mind. And to be honest, a dog could not have made the difference friends and family did during that time. Friends still supported us by caring for John Luke and by including him in golf days and weekend plans. Bill Moretti even continued John Luke's regular lessons for free so that my son could feel that sense of continuity and security in his life.

On the financial front, Jerry made two petitions to the court during this time: The first was a request to lower the price of the house. I was disappointed because every penny we got from its sale meant one more for the creditors, but interest wasn't high for such an expensive piece of real estate. Our showings were few and repeat showings almost nonexistent.

And Jerry petitioned for the mortgage payments to

be made from the estate account. This too felt like a defeat as, again, every penny spent meant one less for the creditors. But money was running low, and I still refused to default on the mortgage payments.

The court granted permission to lower the price on the house. Nevertheless, I really didn't think I could live within it another day. I would continue to pay for it, but I just couldn't live there. It felt increasingly oppressive. I also wasn't sure how I was going to pay for where we might live. Mark's parents and mine still helped me make ends meet.

The court also granted permission to pay the final mortgage payments from the estate account until the house sold. Yes, Mark's insurance policy from work had paid out to me, but I reserved that for legal bills. I also wanted to keep as much as possible if a portion of it was needed for the creditors.

I, who had always been the giver of gifts and had loved my role as hostess, was now the recipient of tremendous and sacrificial generosity, and enduring care—I couldn't bear to ask for more. I couldn't bear to need more. Many friends who had gone through cancer told me how hard it was to receive for prolonged periods of time, but I hadn't felt it firsthand until I started counting this journey not in days or weeks, but in months. Additionally, I was so overwhelmed with all that was happening, I couldn't even plan a next step to make moving out of our house a reality. I thought, until the house sold, John Luke and I were trapped within it.

Here God showed His hand again, working through the hearts and minds of good people. Jeff Stedman called one afternoon. "Go find a house," he said. "Lisa and I have talked to the McNairs and the Jamails. We plan to purchase a house as an investment through an LLC, and you can live in it rent-free until John Luke graduates from high school. You will only need to pay the taxes and insurance, and cover any expenses for maintenance."

He then told me the three couples had already formed and named their limited liability corporation Pro327 after Proverbs 3:27: *Do not withhold good from those to whom it is due, when it is in your power to act.*

"I can't do that," I replied.

"It's not up for discussion. You're going to have to learn to accept things from people. Go find the house you want and we'll take it from there."

Even though Jeff Stedman was Mark's best friend, he was also my close friend—like a second brother to me. Lisa and Mark had often shaken their heads at Jeff and me—we were similar in so many ways. That he would show us such love humbled me. I realized then that as much as I couldn't understand the pain Mark carried, I didn't know or understand the pain Jeff carried. My mind flashed back to a meeting we'd had soon after Mark died. Jeff and I sat in Monte's office as Monte relayed Mark's final call to him. "Right before he hung up, Mark said he had to call his wife and best friend."

I shook my head in tears. "I'm a sucky best friend." I

had thought it was one call, that Mark was referring to me as both wife and best friend.

Jeff shook his head. "No, Becky. Not one call. Two. *I'm* the sucky best friend."

Yet Jeff didn't retreat into his pain; he stepped out. He flew from Colorado Springs the night Mark died, and for every moment after, he worked to care for the kids and me.

But this unbelievable generosity to buy my family a house floored me. And the fact that the McNairs and the Jamails joined him humbled me further—especially since I still owed the Stedmans $225,000 and the Jamails $143,000.

So I found a house, and Pro327 made an offer. The house's owner countered at very near the original asking price, which I felt was too high to chase. I began to look for another house. Yet in another crazy "God thing" non-coincidence, Lisa, who lived in Colorado Springs, had previously worked with the owner's Realtor in sales years before. They ran into each other one day and, while catching up, Lisa told her the story of the LLC and my story without mentioning my name. Within days, the counteroffer was withdrawn and Pro327's original offer was accepted. With that news, a wonderful letter arrived from the owner, addressed to me by name. He had done some research and put all the details together. He knew exactly who I was and my situation, and his sweet note relayed that he wanted to be a part of and not a "hindrance to God's providence for a widow."

He also included a thorough description of the house's personality and a list of its quirks.

I was thrilled and received court permission to move into the new house the last week of October. As I prepared for moving day, I was overwhelmed again—this time by the number of people who showed up to help me move. Friends knew I wanted to keep my expenses to a minimum, and they came in cars and trucks to move everything but the very large pieces. My brother Johnny came from Houston and stayed with me, working for days to do the heavy lifting. Two creditors came to help, and even some of David Gonzales's men's Bible study came one afternoon to load and unload boxes. Monte also showed up—the time he gave never showed up in his billing, like many of the hours he worked on my behalf.

I sent John Luke to his grandparents' that weekend so that I could unpack in the new house and make his room perfect upon his return. I wanted him to feel like he was *coming* home rather than fleeing home. I didn't want to add any new stress to his life.

After two full days of moving, sorting, and unpacking, it looked pretty good. I sank into an armchair in my bedroom my first night in the house. John Luke would arrive the next afternoon. The doorbell rang. I popped up and headed to answer it.

David and Christie Gonzales stood on my front stoop. Christie was wearing her pajamas. "I don't want you to be alone tonight," she said.

She was devastated we'd had to move. She was

heartbroken at all we were going through, and she was worried about me because she knew my past fears of being alone. But I had no fear. I felt nothing but peace and release in my new home. They came in for a while, and we visited. Then I thanked them, hugged them, and sent them home. Then I headed to bed.

The new house lifted me. I took my nightly bubble bath, listened to some country music, and slept well. That next morning I woke to an unbelievable Austin skyline sunrise. Although many aspects of my journey had not changed, the move was a glorious step forward. I now had a view of downtown Austin that felt open and expansive. It felt like God was breathing into my lungs. And now I didn't have to face the questions, the doubt, and the weight of the past every time I opened a cabinet, a drawer, or a closet.

Soon after moving, I awoke early one morning in darkness to see the bright lights of the Zilker Park Christmas tree out my bedroom window. Workers were constructing it in the predawn hours. For a long time I sat and watched as lights were added and lit to form Austin's iconic tree. I didn't have my usual thirteen-foot tree anymore; I had the 155-foot-tall Zilker Park tree! Once again, God was saying: *I am here.*

My lawyers held a second creditors' meeting on November 1. It was important to summarize where we were and where we were headed. I wasn't allowed to attend, so I waited anxiously to hear how it went with the creditors. Bill outlined to the creditors what he had written in his previous email, that the final forensic accounting number had come in at $21.5 million and that Invesco had immediately repaid $5.1 million to their clients. Mark's estate would pay the $16.4 million balance. Bill also stated that, with the official death certificate, we had secured $10 million of the insurance proceeds, and funds sat protected at Prosperity Bank. He noted one creditor had not yet relinquished his lien on the remaining $5 million policy, so those monies could not yet be included in our totals, but they too sat safely in a court-controlled account.

While that final detail caused a stir in the room, Bill kept going. He informed the creditors that we had reduced the price of the house and confirmed my intention to place those proceeds into the estate for their repayment. He then explained that we were now ready to file with the IRS, noting "the IRS decision to take a backseat to the creditors is crucial to accomplish a resolution of this matter."

He repeated his warning that Invesco had filed a claim against me for the $5.1 million it paid to Atlantic Trust's clients. "We expected this. They will release their claim to the money, we understand, when a global settlement agreement has been reached. But we also need you to understand that in rejecting that claim, we expect a lawsuit. You should expect to see that, too."

His warning was purposeful. This was procedural. Without doubt Invesco would sue me, and we needed to make sure everyone understood that. There had already been grumbling about suing Invesco, and we were nervous that once lawyers, who watched every move, found the lawsuit filed in court, Invesco's action might very well start the avalanche of lawsuits we had so far avoided.

Many within the room raised their voices in anger once again, either to sue Invesco in retaliation or to sue me to grab a piece of the estate before it shrunk substantially.

Bill again cautioned calm and measured steps. He stated my request that no one sue Invesco and that everyone wait on me. He even announced that my kids were willing to give up everything as well, including John Luke's signed prized jerseys. Frank Ikard wasn't so calm or measured. He stood up and barked at the room, "You all don't get it. She doesn't have to do this and give you these funds." His words quieted the room immediately. I learned of this only as emails starting arriving at my lawyers' offices soon after the meeting:

Dear Jerry,

Just a note to express my sincere appreciation for what you and the Becky Powell team are doing to arrive at the potential of a very fair settlement. It is always interesting as to how the "quibble factor" escalates when you have a room full of lawyers. Frank's explanation at the end was perfect and priceless at forcing the attendees to understand the gift horse concept. I am pleased and impressed that his brief statement did more to encourage reason than almost anything else said. You tell him I said so. And thanks for your efforts.

Another note arrived days later:

To: Bill Jones

Fr: John Needham

Bill, I know you to be a Christian (as well as Becky), and that is the only explanation I can find for the miracle that you (and your team) have pulled off here! In my mind anything close to what you have outlined will be an amazing outcome, well beyond what, at least the lending alumni I have spoken with, ever expected. My hat is off to you, and to be honest it was all I could do not to stand up in the meeting on Nov. 1 and tell off the lawyers in the room to quit looking for an angle and go give you a high five...

Greatly appreciate you, and the incredible work you have done here for us and for Becky. It is a phenomenal testimony!

A lot happened during that fairly brief meeting, and it was a miracle no one got jumpy and filed a lawsuit following it. Again, I believe God placed a few very level heads in that room, including those on the shoulders of my lawyers. A few creditors did band together in the following days and inform Bill that if Invesco sued me, they would sue Invesco. I was touched by their loyalty, but I asked Bill and each of my lawyers to call everyone within the group and beg them not to do that. Many creditors and their lawyers believed Invesco was liable as Mark's employer and wanted to sue, especially since Mark had pledged Invesco stock to secure his loans, and Invesco carried a $25 million insurance policy to cover such situations.

Suing Invesco felt to many like a viable option. And the creditors wanted action; it often feels better than waiting. But a case against Invesco was not cut-and-dried, and the first lawsuit filed against them would start a battle. My lawyers made calls and sent countless emails urging creditors not to "fire the first bullet," and to instead stand by their filings against Mark's estate.

We filed our statement with the IRS on November 17, 2013. I had wanted it filed months before. Now, rather than March, my payout day would be May 8, 2015. It was too far away, but it was the best it could be. With that waiting period as our guiding strategy, we began working on the release, the "Global Settlement Agreement," which each creditor would sign on May 8 in order to get repaid. My lawyers also made the final determination about clawbacks during this time. My tax attorney was adamant. "Absolutely not. We will not do that." We would not pursue them. It was the final word on the issue. And I couldn't help sending a smug *I got my way* look across the table. Jerry, Bill, and Monte rolled their eyes and moved on to the next topic.

At this point, one might say the story could end. We had an end date, and my intentions were clear. The clawback issue was settled. The IRS had eighteen months to decide on our paperwork. If all went well, and no one sued in the meantime, the creditors could be paid on May 8. Clear and simple. Done and dusted. But so much could go wrong within those eighteen months.

The pressure was unrelenting. I'd been at this daily grind for seven months by this time and felt completely worn out, and still grief-stricken. And now I had eighteen more months ahead of me. I wasn't sure I could endure eighteen more months, so I continued to search for loopholes around the long waiting period.

It's hard to explain, especially as the days grew dark earlier and the holidays approached, how bleak everything felt. It wasn't despair. I was learning to hold peace within my heart, knowing that God was working "all things toward good" (Romans 8:28), without actually feeling it. But I was beaten down, discouraged.

One day late in the fall, Lisa called from Colorado Springs. "I haven't talked to you in a while. You haven't called me."

"Then pick up the f%&*@#! phone and call *me* if you

want to talk," I snapped. "With all I have going on, do you even think I can remember who I talk to?"

Silence lay between us.

We hung up soon after that. Indignation fueled me for a while, but as I dropped into the bathtub that night I was so ashamed of myself. Not only had I added another F word to my list, one I'm not proud of, but I had also abused a friend. I felt so worn out, frustrated, and torn. Criminal charges against me were still a prospect—the FBI was still culling information gleaned from Mark's personal and work files. And the IRS was a constant, considerable concern.

I was also saddened at how I had changed. I once was the friend who reached out, the friend who initiated lunches and fun and phone calls. I was the host friends came to for that glass of wine and that long, relaxed talk in the evening.

I wasn't capable of being that person at this time— not because I didn't want to be that friend, but because I didn't have the ability to be that friend. I didn't have the time, the energy, or the bandwidth to handle one more thing. It was unintentional that I hadn't called Lisa, and it was also true I was so shredded most days I couldn't remember who I had spoken to or what we had said. If I didn't feel sad in any given moment it was only because I felt numb and overwhelmed. It was also true that I had taken Lisa for granted, which made me realize how many other friends I'd taken for granted. I lay down in the bath, saddened and ashamed, yet glad to be reminded that in the midst of a crisis, as much as I needed grace, I needed to give it as well.

When I climbed out of the bath, I called Lisa to apologize.

I was reminded too how important my lawyers had become to me. Not only were they working hard to unwind my legal and financial mess, but they had also become good and dependable friends, and pretty much the only people I could turn to and honestly share my reality. Just before Thanksgiving, I wrote them a note to express my appreciation, ending it with Philippians 1:3: *I thank my God every time I remember you.*

Soon after I sent the letter, Thanksgiving arrived with both pain and blessings. The kids and I drove to Houston to spend it with my family. My parents, sister, and brother all live in Houston, and we often gathered there for Thanksgiving. In the past, Mark had always said the prayer over the meal.

That year, my brother-in-law looked to Boone as we held hands around the table to say grace. "Boone, will you say the prayer?" he asked.

Boone nodded, bowed his head, and started to pray aloud. About halfway through, he started crying and ended the prayer in a start-stop sob. I quietly hugged him afterward before we sat and ate.

When dinner was over, my brother-in-law found me in the kitchen. "I'm sorry I put him on the spot like that."

"No." I reached for Johnny's hand. "I'm so glad he's

showing emotion and he's okay crying. He's worked so hard to be the man of the family. But he needs to know it's okay to be sad." Boone, my middle child, my peacemaker and stoic citizen, had carried so much. So while it hurt to see him hurting, it was also good to see Boone open up and express his pain. It was the next step for him. It was a next step for all of us.

And though Thanksgiving is wonderful, for me it is really a gateway to Christmas, always and forever my favorite time of the year. My ringtone remains a Christmas carol throughout the year, and I count down the days with an app all year long. Returning from Houston after Thanksgiving, we found the house already set for Christmas. I had decorated it before leaving so as not to miss a moment of the "most wonderful season of all." Each year, the living room's centerpiece was the fireplace mantel with garland draped across it and all five stockings hanging in a row. But this year the kids noted right away that my stocking was not hanging with theirs on the mantel. I just couldn't hang mine, not without Mark's next to it. It was too heartbreaking.

The beginning of the Christmas season also made me immediately think of our yearly Christmas party held the first Wednesday in December. That first Wednesday I woke up feeling as if my name was in the air. But I was no longer living in that house, and I certainly couldn't afford the party anymore. Life had changed dramatically; that "season" had passed.

My friends understood and showed up, without my

ever saying a word. To lift my spirits, right after Thanks-giving they inflated the forty-foot Frosty the Snowman in my front yard. He hadn't been seen since July when we'd blown him up inside David Wise's office. But there he was—bigger than my new house, tucked tight in my small yard. I felt very blessed the homeowners' associa-tion didn't issue a citation! And on the first Wednesday in December, a few of them planned a mini-party and supplied the food. We sat around my kitchen table that evening, talking of Christmases past and Christmases yet to come.

While I wasn't anticipating all the joys of our normal Christmas celebrations and was thankful for new tradi-tions, I still didn't expect Invesco's suit to arrive before the holidays. But on December 13, Invesco filed suit against me. I understand that they did it to protect themselves, but I was devastated. I had stood between it and the creditors, by asking each and every creditor to wait for me to pay them and not pursue Invesco, and yet Invesco not only sued me, but their lawyers also told me to sue ABC Bank, which Mark had used for creditor transactions. ABC Bank was the one that sued Invesco right after Mark died, since he had offered Invesco stock as collateral for his loan from the bank. Invesco's suggestion infuriated me. ABC Bank's presi-dent was a good and kind man trying to do the right thing, and lawsuits were exactly what I was working tirelessly to avoid.

I could hardly speak for days, which is very unusual

for me, but probably a good thing. It reminds me of the old saying: If you can't say something kind, don't say anything at all. I did my best not to express my frustration and anger. But when a friend finally asked how I felt about the suit, a reply came to me. It was not gracious, but it was true: "I'm praying for them just like 'Pray for You' by Jaron says." After all, it *was* the first song I listened to in my bubble bath on December 13 and for a few nights after. It's a wonderful tongue-in-cheek song that describes a man praying for another the only way he can at that moment, with verses like "I pray a flowerpot falls from a windowsill and knocks you in the head like I'd like to." It was not one of my better moments; I certainly wasn't behaving in a forgiving manner.

However, there was a tiny bit of light on December 13: Invesco officially informed my lawyers that it would forgo its claim for the $5.1 million against Mark's estate if our settlement agreement with the creditors released Invesco from all future claims. The suit was procedural, a form of corporate protection, and I understood that. It didn't please me, but it made sense.

And God was certainly active that day. That very evening, Jeff organized a group of men to celebrate John Luke's thirteenth birthday. When Boone turned thirteen, Mark hosted a dinner with his close friends to surround Boone with men he could look up to and emulate. It was a beautiful evening that Boone cherished. Now those same men came together to provide the celebratory dinner and the enduring support for John Luke. Each man wrote John Luke a letter, and each man remains a guiding influence in his life today.

The days marched on, and Christmas arrived. I want to say I embraced it and felt joy, but it felt dark and sad. Not only was the pressure unrelenting, but also my husband had been an integral part of so many of our traditions. He was the one who would get up extra early Christmas Day to light the fire in the fireplace, turn on all of the lights, and set the stage for Christmas morning. He was the one who called upstairs to the kids when it was time to come down. He was the one who got excited with the gifts they received and the memories they would soon make together playing with them—mostly golf-related equipment for the boys. Although the last seven months had changed my view of our marriage, there was still so much good to remember.

Someone asked during this time if I still loved Mark, especially with all we were going through. I did. My heart broke for the pain he must have been carrying. I will never know what his inner world was like, even though I lived, walked, and slept beside him for more than twenty-two years. That broke my heart, too—and continues to hurt today.

During our marriage, Mark carried most of the pressures of life. He had handled all our finances, decisions, and concerns. After these seven months, I was growing weary of the load. Daily I had to recommit to the choice I'd made to move forward. It often feels so tempting and so easy to slip into the past, rethink, dwell, and condemn. Sometimes it feels good to savor our hurts and lick our wounds. There's a satisfaction in it. But again each day, as I showered and put on my makeup, I made the conscious decision to keep stepping forward and not look back. Philippians 3:13–14 helped with that: *Brothers and sisters, I do not consider myself yet to have taken hold of it. But one thing I do: Forgetting what is behind straining toward what is ahead, I press on toward the goal to win the prize for which God has called me heavenward in Christ Jesus.* It was the perfect rallying cry to face forward, and forgive and forget what lay behind.

I was still under investigation for criminal involvement, so I could only bring this pain and this commitment to God. It truly was a time of intense prayer and waiting—a time for "me and God."

That said, so many blessings occurred in this holy and beautiful time as well. On December 23, I was home baking—making pound cakes, which I now do every Christmas—when the doorbell rang. Friends filed into my living room. I was so happy to see them and delighted they dropped by to cheer my day. Then they stepped aside to reveal a bench sitting on the porch. They knew I visited Mark's grave and wanted me to have a place to sit beside it. I burst into tears and buried my face in Melissa's shoulder, swamped with a feeling beyond gratitude.

A few days after Christmas, I became overwhelmed by gratitude again. I was tired after a long day of meetings and dropped my bag on the kitchen counter. No one else was home, and the house was dark. Turning toward the large kitchen window, light caught my eye. The kitchen window in my new home had a full east view over the growing Austin skyline. I looked out and saw, at that moment, the sky filled with a magnificent rainbow. Rainbows have always been a sign of God's promise and His faithfulness to me, from as far back as my mom singing "Somewhere Over the Rainbow" to me in childhood. Since Mark's death I noticed them more frequently and at significant moments, moments when I needed God. Here at my lowest, my friends and God had met me. They'd given me a bench and He had given me a rainbow. I took out my phone and snapped a picture so I could remember it. The picture was gorgeous, each color sharp and clear.

I am here, He said again.

Chapter 10

When darkness comes to town, I'm a lighter, get out
aliver, of the fire, survivor. I'm a riser.

—"Riser" by Dierks Bentley

Christmas came and went, and the new year did not
bring the lift it usually does.

I often sit down at the beginning of the new year and
think about the blank slate ahead and what it might
hold. We couldn't pay the creditors until May 8, 2015,
so 2014 seemed to stretch ahead like a black cloud. And
Mark wasn't there for our usual anniversary trip. In our
twenty-two years of marriage, we had missed only one,
when John Luke was born.

An email from that time expresses more how I felt
than anything I might say here:

January 8, 2014

Bill and Monte,

I am so sorry that I was so upset today. I understand this is going to take time and considering all the people involved and the incredibly huge mess this is, I should not complain. I promise to be more patient in the future. You both have done an amazing job and I know you are doing everything you can to make it easier for me. I want to make clear that I have not changed my mind about what we are doing. I was just trying to think of ways to make it happen faster. It is emotionally exhausting. I am sure you say that about me too.

There is no doubt in my mind at all about how you are handling the situation. I know you both are doing the right thing and giving me the best advice available anywhere! I know because I truly believe that God put you both in this situation and my life on that day because you are the right Godly men for the job (you will have to take that up with Him yourselves).

I wish I could have come to the conclusion that I need to be more patient and that this is going to take time before our meeting today. As you can see, God still has a lot of work left to do on me! Wish I could figure that out too.

Love you both!

Even Eddie Safady noted I was running out of steam in the new year: "Everyone thought you would crumble. We were waiting for the breakdown."

Patience had never been my strong suit—and clearly I was not growing in that gift fast enough. In fact, one day I pushed Monte so hard he got frustrated and didn't talk to me for three days. He needed a break from me, and I couldn't blame him—sometimes I need a break from myself.

During our days of silence, I took matters to the next level. I baked a pound cake for my apology and drafted my first and only legal document. Mary Beth and Ben—also an attorney, but not on my payroll—helped me.

I agreed to wait patiently and not pester my lawyers, as best I could, if they signed the following document and agreed to my terms…But first I pressed one last time!

Dear Bill, Monte, and Johnny,

I have been thinking and praying about waiting until May 8, 2015 (please note it is two days before my 49th birthday), and I still do not feel at peace about waiting. Not that I am ready to full on pursue the IRS either; I have no doubt that you all are doing absolutely everything, but I still have questions.

Have ALL the possibilities of paying the creditors now and not waiting the fifteen months been explored? Is the IRS the final word, or is there another entity that trumps the IRS? Could Judge Herman ask the IRS to let us pay creditors? Can we come up with something new and creative? I would feel better if we could take a few more days to explore options to be sure there is not another way to pay the creditors back sooner.

I don't want to frustrate you all, but you know I want to get the creditors paid back sooner than later. In the event we do wait it out for fifteen months I am prepared. I have attached a document for you all to sign. I have been spending way too much time with attorneys and I needed a little humor; clearly I need to get out more.

I wrote up a nine-page "legal" document calling my lawyers out as "The Three Wise Men" and pledging myself to patience. And if I delivered on that patience, and didn't pester them relentlessly until May 8, 2015, there were a few terms they needed to meet as well.

1. Jones shall purchase, because of his impeccable taste in women's footwear, for Powell footwear of his choice (which footwear must be acceptable to Powell, in her sole discretion, without regard to price, style, color, design, or otherwise, and without regard to whether such footwear consists of heels, boots, sandals, slippers, wooden clogs, or any other footwear of whatever kind with the exception of athletic footwear), when she feels like it, in perpetuity, or until such mental and emotional anguish and distress drives Powell to her grave.

2. James shall purchase for Powell one firearm of his choice (which firearm must be acceptable to Powell, in her discretion, without regard to price, style, color, design, or otherwise, and without regard to whether such firearm is a pistol, handgun, shotgun, assault rifle, or otherwise), on an annual basis, in perpetuity, or until such mental and emotional anguish and distress drives Powell to her grave. Please note, Powell promises not to shoot The Three Wise Men with said firearms.

3. Sutton shall provide Powell and each of her children a "Get Out of Jail Free" card in perpetuity for any and all future criminal acts that Powell is driven to commit as a result of such additional mental and emotional anguish and distress that she is forced to endure during such additional fifteen (15) month period, as well as all crimes that each of her children may be compelled to commit as a result of Powell's mental and emotional anguish and distress. Such full legal representation shall also include full legal representation with respect to any commitment proceedings initiated by the State of Texas' Office of Mental Health and Rehabilitation, and any medical costs incurred as a result of any such commitment.

I also added a section that granted me a spa day if waiting brought the press around. Drafting the document was an amazing and fun endeavor that kept me smiling for days. While I won't confirm or deny my lawyers signed said agreement, I will state I received a fantastic pair of bright pink Yves Saint Laurent heels and a gift certificate for a gun, if I chose to purchase one. I have yet to receive anything resembling a "get out of jail free" card and suspect I never will.

Despite the frustrations in waiting until May 2015, there was plenty to keep me busy in the meantime. In January, the house—after two price reductions—finally sold. Once again, I was stunned by the generosity of others.

Two friends of mine who are Realtors handled the sale. They each gave up their commissions so that more money could go to the estate to pay creditors. And not only that—the buyer didn't have a Realtor so those fees went to my Realtors, who released those as well. There were no fees for the house's sale!

One of my Realtors had to appear in court to personally state this intention. "You all are waiving your fees? That's six percent of the sale." The judge's voice was filled with incredulity.

"Yes, Judge." She nodded.

He shook his head and with a small smile turned to me. "You really do have some amazing friends."

"Yes, Judge," was all I could say.

Again and again, in so many ways, through so many people, God showed His grace and generosity.

That very day, I began clearing the house in earnest.

Although much of it was hard, some of it was funny, too—in that strange way that struck me at times. This is where we found those books in Mark's study I told you about, and it was during this time that Kate had her "God thing" moment and told me I would trust and love again. So again, mixed with the pain of an ending, God brought friends and laughter into the hard places.

It also surprised me, as I dug into every corner of the house, how much we'd collected over the years and how little I wanted or needed to keep. My views of stuff and money had changed. It now felt aligned with another song I enjoyed during this time, "What You Give Away" by Vince Gill and Sheryl Crow: "All you can take is what you give away." It goes on to talk about what matters in life and the importance of hitting our knees and praying, and what we hope to say at the end of our lives about how we used our time and resources. On Judgment Day, I do not want to point to my "stuff."

But as the court "owned" everything that belonged to me, I needed permission to sell or dispose of anything I didn't want to keep. I asked Jerry what to do. He canvassed the Three Wise Men (as created in my "legal" document above).

Becky proposed to have a garage sale to dispose of certain tangible personal property that has little value. Some of her friends have agreed to oversee the sale. Technically, we need permission to sell anything,

even this stuff, or even to give it away. But Becky
does need to do something with these items and to
store them is a lot of cost. Becky reminded me that
you guys are sending out an email to creditors soon.
Do you think it wise to inform them?

A rapid-fire email conversation ensued...

Monte: I'm worried about creditors seeing the application and saying, oh yeah, what about all that nice valuable stuff in the house?

Jerry: At the same time, Becky needs to do something with it before the house closes.

Bill: I share your concerns. If it's a small sum, Becky might consider giving it away. If it is larger, we should at least visit about it.

Monte: Giving it away without permission troubles me.

Jerry: I meant with court approval.

It went on until I finally had enough and chimed in: I was thinking about soaking in a bubble bath tonight. Does anybody have a problem with that or do I need to ask Judge Herman first?

Only Jerry replied: Fellows... It looks like she has gone daft on us as we go down the stretch.

I had agreed to wait with patience. I had drafted a "legal" document pledging myself to patience. Yet I felt no patience or peace about the decision. I understood we were waiting for the IRS to subrogate their rights in favor of repaying the creditors, but waiting still felt as though I was protecting my interests and not the creditors.

God laid Philippians 2:3–4 on my heart in a strong way that spring: *Do nothing out of selfish ambition or vain conceit. Rather, in humility value others above yourselves, not looking to your own interests but each of you to the interests of the others.*

So despite my legal document and my resolution of patience, I couldn't help myself—I pushed my lawyers for new thinking. I asked my same questions again: *Have all the possibilities to repay the creditors now been explored? Is the IRS the final word? Could Judge Herman ask the IRS to let us repay the creditors?*

While those questions consumed my prayer time and my meetings, other aspects of my life moved forward. Valentine's Day drew closer. On Valentine's Day eve friends invited me to dinner at Uchi. During our meal, David Gonzales, David Wise, Corey Ray, and Mark Adams pulled out a pink gift bag and set it on the table in front of me. Inside I found a card, a pink stuffed lion holding a heart that said "Wild About You," and a beautiful Baccarat crystal heart. These four men had organized this gift for me without even discussing it with their wives. While their wives could not have been more touched than I was by their husbands' sensitivity and generosity, they were definitely impressed. In fact, whenever my dear friends whine about these husbands

now, I say, "Yes, but remember that Valentine's Day..."
It gets them smiling every time.

While dinner was far more than I expected that
Valentine's Day, there was more to come. Late that night
I heard John Luke in the kitchen after we had both
gone to bed.

"Are you okay out there?" I called from my room,
on the first floor next to the kitchen. His room is
above mine.

"I just came down for a glass of water."

I woke at five the next morning for prayer time and
coffee and found two dozen white roses, chocolates
and caramels, and a beautiful homemade card on the
kitchen counter. Mark had always given me two dozen
white roses. This year John Luke asked Melissa to help
him take care of all the details for a perfect gift. Beyond
that, Boone and John Luke remembered their sister as
well. The usual pink roses Mark had always given to
Madison each Valentine's Day arrived, too—but from
her brothers. The thoughtfulness of my boys brought
me to tears again.

And that was just the beginning of Valentine's
Day... At noon, Madison surprised me by driving from
Baylor for a lunch at Chrissy Ray's house. She too knew
it would be a hard day for me and had organized, with
the help of my friends, a fun luncheon.

Life was moving forward in so many ways. It was
different, but little bits of what I did and who I was
began to return. Later that month, Dinah invited me to

Mexico for a weekend to celebrate her husband's fiftieth birthday. A few close friends were going, and the idea of sun and rest and getting away from Austin for a few days appealed to me. I asked for permission.

Am I allowed to leave the country? I have a friend celebrating her husband's 50th birthday in Mexico and I'd like to go. I thought I should ask before I potentially got stopped at the airport.

Again a volley of emails made the rounds:

Bill: I can't think of any reason you can't go. You should probably plan on returning at some point.

Me: Do I have to?

Monte: No, but pick somewhere better to escape to.

Johnny: You guys obviously have not been to Puerto Escondido.

Bill: We don't get out much.

The emails reflect the lighter tone we shared. The sun was shining more, and we felt upbeat. While my lawyers still worked hard on the details, we were in a holding pattern. Waiting for May 8, 2015, and the IRS to give precedence to the creditors still guided our strategy and actions. The creditors seemed to be in it with us, waiting patiently, and the government agencies continued with their investigations. Although none of them had closed their investigations on me, they hadn't actively pursued me, either. After searching my house in June with incredible care and discretion, the FBI had not even requested an interview. It had become so clear in all the documents recovered and all the interviews conducted that I knew nothing of Mark's dealings.

Then...on February 27, the FBI closed its criminal investigation against me. For nine months, I had lived with the burden, and I felt its painful weight daily, that I could go to jail. To have that lifted from my shoulders...Well, let's just say it felt like I grew two inches that day.

Chapter 11

I got my high heels on with my boxing gloves . . . I might
fall down, but I get back up.

—"Fight Like a Girl" by Kalie Shorr

Although I'd been a widow almost a year by that next
spring, I still found that everyday things brought up
memories at the most unexpected times. I never knew
when the feeling of loss would overtake me and I would
end up in a puddle of sadness, at the drugstore, the
school parking lot, or the grocery store.

Mark had a few things he always cooked for us.
"Dad's Spegeht" was a family favorite. While it took the
average person about a half hour to boil pasta and pour
a jar of sauce over it, it took Mark hours. He would
purchase three different shapes of pasta and mix them,
then use two different jars of sauce and simmer them
down. He then served it to the kids with a flourish that
made them feel he'd handed them a five-star dinner.

One day I reached for a box of pasta at the grocery store and remembered those dinners. I started crying again in aisle five.

Madison turned twenty-one that spring. We had held extravagant celebrations for sweet sixteens and those all-important eighteenth birthdays. But here was my eldest child reaching the milestone of twenty-one. What was I to do? Our financial situation—our every situation—was so different from what we had expected for this day.

In the end, I chose to give her Mark's wedding band. The police gave it back to me the day after he died, and I decided not to bury it with him. Inside, I had inscribed our wedding date, December 8, 1990, and 1 Corinthians 13:4: *Love is patient, love is kind. It does not envy, it does not boast, it is not proud.* It felt right to give Madison this precious memento that had belonged to her father and remind her of the love I hoped would guide her every day of her life. So though it was an emotional day, my daughter's twenty-first birthday was a very good day.

As spring continued to warm toward summer, I felt a lift every day from no longer having an open FBI file. I no longer feared jail. Only when they closed their investigation did I fully realize how heavily that possibility had weighed on me. It truly felt that each day I straightened and opened a little more. I still had open SEC and DOJ files, but they concerned me less. Johnny, my criminal attorney, felt those investigations didn't signal anything ominous. He suspected both agencies were waiting until creditors were repaid. *Yeah, me too!*

Johnny gave me permission to attend the birthday celebration in Mexico—which made April a month of firsts for me.

The Mexico trip was my first trip in almost a year and my first trip, outside visiting family, without Mark. It meant a lot to me. It is a strange thing to explain to someone how that feels—to have open investigations against you, to have to ask the court for money to pay your water bill, to not be able to throw or give anything away, to ask permission to travel a few miles south for a birthday party, and to do that, for the first time, without your husband, who had been an integral part of every trip.

I had never fully understood the term "surrender" before this time, but I was learning it on multiple levels. The idea of "surrendering" to God had always felt ephemeral to me, a constant struggle, but one without substance to grasp or dire consequences to endure. Eternal ideas took on concrete realities in my world now. I realized how little I really controlled. We often think of our property as our own, our work as our own, even our time. But none of it is—I controlled none of those things. My sense of control had been an illusion. I clung to Psalm 25:4–5: *Show me your ways, Lord, teach me your paths. Guide me in your truth and teach me, for you are God my Savior, and my hope is in you all day long.* I wanted, as I ventured further into this new life, for each step to be within His will, fully dependent on His care.

I savored the warmth of Mexico in April. It felt like life was gently unfurling. One night at dinner a friend turned to me and said, "So...are you ready to start dating?"

His wife raised her eyebrows, as did I. The question surprised me. Not because I hadn't been asked out— three men had already posed the same question, one two months after Mark died and one via text. But was I *ready*? My mind cast back to my conversation with Kate. I still loved Mark, and I had no better answer now than I did for Kate. "I doubt I'll ever trust another man," I said.

My friend sat back and considered me. "The odds are in your favor, you know. If you think about it, it's unlikely another man will do that or that anything worse can happen to you."

I burst out laughing. That was certainly one way to look at it.

I also went to my first movie later in April—with girlfriends, no men invited.

Kathy Smith knew I needed a laugh one day and suggested I grab a friend and go see the romantic comedy *The Other Woman*. She said it was light, adorable, and everything I needed to lift my spirits.

Christie, Jill, Melissa, and I went that afternoon. I was excited to do something as normal as going to the movies.

I'm not sure if you've seen *The Other Woman*, starring Cameron Diaz, Leslie Mann, and Kate Upton, but let me break it down for you—this movie Kathy found light and delightful. Mark, the main character, is a financier who is defrauding clients and cheating on his wife. His wife teams up with Mark's two mistresses to not only trap him in his affairs, but also end his criminal financial dealings. Then the three of them (Diaz plays a lawyer) work to legally pay back every penny he has stolen.

I sat throughout the show vacillating between tears, laughter, and jaw-dropping incredulity. My three friends sat silent and shocked beside me. At one point, Melissa reached for my hand and whispered, "Are you okay?"

When I laid the plot out for Kathy, she was horrified. "I didn't realize," she said.

That made me laugh even more.

May 16, 2014, soon arrived. It was the first anniversary of Mark's death, and I wanted to honor the day with family and friends, not only as a way to remember Mark, but to come together and thank them for their support throughout the year. I hosted a picnic at Mark's grave.

About sixty of us gathered that evening, and the kids lit a large paper lantern in a moving tribute as the sky darkened. But the wind caught the lantern and drove it down rather than up into the sky!

Ever the lawyer, Monte freaked out. "It's going to start a fire. There's going to be a lawsuit. You do not need that right now. The publicity is going to be horrible."

My nephew Joey took off running through the neighborhood to find the lantern and bring it back. He soon returned with the lantern. The scare was averted, and we didn't light another. Instead, we spent the rest of the evening chatting, sharing stories, and enjoying "Mark's Margaritas," which the Gonzaleses brought pre-made.

At the end of the evening, I stood to thank everyone for their extraordinary support and friendship. I included two verses in my thank-you, starting with the second half of Job 1:21. *"The Lord gave and the Lord has taken away; may the name of the Lord be praised."* I needed to share this verse for so many reasons. Yes, my family had experienced incredible loss in that year, but we had also been blessed beyond measure. We had been shown extraordinary grace and love, both from God and from all the friends present that afternoon— and it would be wrong to accept God's gifts without his sovereignty over the loss.

I then read the next verse, the first half of Job 2:10, where Job replied, *"You are talking like a foolish woman. Shall we accept good from God, and not trouble?"* Job was speaking against his wife, who wanted him to curse God for the tragedy that had befallen them. I had found such wisdom and comfort in Job's reply. My kids and I were learning to pray and praise in all circumstances. We would be "foolish" and hypocritical to accept from God blessings with one hand and raise the other in angry protest when things didn't go our way.

I also shared with everyone the enormous peace I felt. I then read to them an entry from my *Jesus Calling: 365 Devotions for Kids* from the month before. The reading had struck me, and I'd bookmarked it just for this day. The devotional began with a description of God's daily provision of manna for the Israelites in the desert. It then went on to say, from God's perspective:

> When you come to Me in prayer with a thankful heart, I give you enough Peace for today. I will not give you enough for tomorrow—only today. That is because I want you to come to Me again tomorrow—and each day after that. If I gave you enough Peace to last your whole life, you might fall into the trap of thinking you didn't need Me.

I grew teary as I closed the book and looked out at all those loving faces. At that point, my dad, whom I've called "Baby Friend" since I was a little girl, came to stand behind me. Not only did he not want me to be alone, but I also think he feared I might faint. I didn't, but I was again thankful for his silent and unconditional love.

If I thought I'd learned a lot about God and surrender during this journey, the summer of 2014 taught me more. I leaned on Him in a new way, digging into my Bible every morning. I was worn out, tired, and still uncomfortable in that "waiting place." It was no longer about the fact that I felt no peace about waiting to repay the creditors until May 8, 2015. It was that I felt a strong and growing compulsion that it was not the right thing to do at all. As I think about that summer, I need to add another F word to my list.

FORWARD

I've talked about forward motion a great deal already. I think it deserves such close treatment because it is a very hard thing to do. It is so hard to keep your eyes forward when what's happened in the past knocks you flat. I can't deny that I looked back at times and had questions, so many questions: *Who was Mark? What was real in our marriage? What signs had I missed? How would this all end? Was waiting to pay the creditors right?*

No matter the situation in which we find ourselves, we always have questions. After losing a job, a parent, a child, a dear friend...we go back, we question, we wrestle with God, and sometimes, oftentimes, we want to walk away from it all and sit with those dark musings. It's an odd reality, but it can feel good and necessary to savor them.

Questions are natural and part of our human makeup—so is wrestling with them and with God. We feel more secure when we have control, or the illusion of it, in any aspect of our lives. But rarely can we go back and change what has come before. Many of the questions we ask are unanswerable. That's not to say we shouldn't bring them to God—we should. I found Him fully capable of handling all my fears, frustrations, pain, and agony. He handled anything and everything I brought to or threw at Him.

In those conversations with God I found, and truly believe, that some backward glances lead to learning, understanding, and growth. After all, that's how we learn from our mistakes. But I was faced with the temptation that summer to look back and then convince myself I was still learning. I was so tired and worn. Dwelling on *What happened?* and a million different versions of *why?* felt restful, even soothing.

It wasn't. It never is.

Looking back too long can harm us—it trips us up as we walk forward. I had to make an active choice that I would not dwell on the unanswerable questions and those alluring backward glances. They distanced me from God. I felt it in tangible ways. I also knew I was never going to get those answers, and the asking, begging, and railing would only frustrate me—and put me deep into that F word. Furthermore, begging for answers would only distract me from what I needed to do. Focusing on the past meant I had less energy for the present. And it didn't set a good example for my children.

If I was serious in my early declaration that I wanted to point my kids to God and never be a stumbling block to their loving Him, I couldn't indulge in backward glances. I couldn't wallow there. All that glorious mud found in a good wallow looked pretty inviting. And when I indulged, even for a morning, in all those *what ifs* and *how could hes*, I felt pulled into a mire that coated me with self-righteous anger and paralyzed me from stepping forward.

God was there to help me accept my past and handle my future—in the present. He gave me "my daily bread" and my peace, just as I'd read to the group gathering at Mark's graveside on May 16. I needed to ask for it every day, praise Him every day, and step out of that wading pool of the past every day.

To move forward is imperative, but impossible when our gaze trails behind. We have to fix our eyes not on what is seen but what is unseen, because what is seen is temporary but what is unseen is eternal (2 Corinthians 4:18).

One morning while the kids and I were at Mark's parents' in Colorado Springs for a summer visit, I couldn't shake the conviction that waiting until May 8, 2015, to repay the creditors was wrong. I also couldn't see any way around its necessity. Yet with every breath, I felt I was missing something.

I started poring through all the files in my possession, rereading every court document and every email in hope of finding something, anything, to bring confirmation. I also started researching tax law on the Internet. I know we are all warned not to diagnose ourselves after medical Internet searches, and I am certain we should never glean tax advice from there, either—yet that's exactly what I did. But rather than find answers, I found a mistake. First off, in reading the form submitted to the IRS, I suspected that even after eighteen months *and* an IRS ruling, the creditors still weren't protected from future judgment. Everything in the form implied that waiting for the IRS to rule would not absolutely protect them. In the end, nothing fully protected them. The IRS could come after me, and the IRS could come after them at any time. Then came the mistake: My Social Security number had been transcribed incorrectly onto the form. Our appeal for a ruling was invalid. And if and when we refiled, the eighteen-month waiting period would start over.

I felt panic rise within me. I called Monte with my suspicions. He was calm and matter-of-fact. "Simply call your accountant and see if your Social Security number is wrong and if they think that means we'll have to start the eighteen-month waiting period again," he said.

Calling my accountants only snowballed the problem. The Social Security number was wrong, and other questions were raised, too. I called Monte back to talk with him about all the conflicting information I'd read and received. He tried to convince me that the solution was clear and right in front of me. Then he gave up. "Call the tax attorney yourself. You're reading it wrong."

I did just that, and an hour later, undone even more because I'd heard something new, I called Monte again to relay that conversation.

"We've gotten it all wrong." I laid out what the tax attorney said in sharp words and few breaths.

Monte disagreed.

I pushed back. "I wrote it down. Waiting for the IRS does not one-hundred-percent protect the creditors as we thought, and withholding the money doesn't protect them; it only protects me. I don't care if the IRS comes after me if the money has all been paid out. I'll take that risk. I'll have nothing left. The best for the creditors is to pay now. Call him yourself."

Monte did, and returned to me hours later. What the tax attorney had told me over the past two days was correct, and it was markedly different from what we had been told previously. Unfortunately, this meant that all the tax advice we had been given and planned our strategy against had changed. There were lots of legal reasons I can't begin to relay or even fully understand, but the bottom line was that waiting for the IRS protected me more than the creditors. To pay out the money actually protected the creditors more, since the SEC had laid down legal precedent that creditors took priority over IRS claims. Yet, as a measure of protection, the tax attorney thought we still might need to refile our IRS paperwork and wait another eighteen months.

I wasn't sure I could handle that, and I was fairly sure a number of creditors wouldn't. Now I was freaking out—another F word. I felt certain that if we started all over, went back to the creditors and told them we had made a miscalculation, both in strategy and execution, no one would believe us. Everybody had been calm and patient; they'd done what we'd asked. And the money was sitting in accounts, ready to pay out. And everyone knew it. I was afraid people would start panicking like a few did the week after Mark died when one lawyer, a creditor himself, had solicited creditors to form a consortium to move—either to wait or to sue—in aggregate. Another person, not a creditor, had actually called my father-in-law and told him it was his responsibility to sell his Colorado home to pay off his son's debts, at least as they pertained to his clients.

It felt like I had started a new ticking clock. It beat faster and louder, and it resided in my chest. That sounds overly dramatic, but I did not believe I could survive another eighteen months. It felt as if my life dangled in limbo and I couldn't draw a good deep breath until all was resolved. The panic, which had subsided over the past several months, was tightening in my chest. I had started frantically pacing across my in-laws' front yard during that first call to Monte, and that frenetic motion did not stop for days. I could not sit still; I could not stand still. I was a live wire, pacing and clutching my chest. When would it end?

My Three Wise Men called in the tax experts and

heard so much conflicting advice no one knew what to believe. They too felt the tension. Waiting until May 8, 2015, had been our path—the one we communicated to the creditors and the one everyone had tacitly agreed upon. To jump off that path was dangerous.

I also felt I betrayed the creditors. One creditor had stated in an *Austin American-Statesman* article published soon after Mark's death, "They're saying there's a bunch of insurance and (Powell's) wife was going to give up everything she had (to repay creditors), but I'll believe it when I see it."

His skepticism felt justified now, and all the goodwill we had created would vanish when panic and lawsuits ensued. I would never pay people back, and, like this man, they would believe the worst of me.

While my lawyers worked in Austin, John Luke and I spent a few days with Mary Beth in Estes Park, Colorado, before coming home. I was beyond myself.

"I can't bear it. I can't do this again. I can't start all over. This is never going to end... I can't bear any more," I told her. Mary Beth was worried for me.

Right as I shared my heartbreak with Mary Beth, a light caught my eye. Without another word, we walked outside to the brightest, most vibrant rainbow I had ever seen.

For all my life, I've seen them as personal signs from a loving God. This one felt so clear—God was speaking—and I was quiet enough, having emptied myself to Mary Beth, to hear Him. Although I had panicked, doubted, and feared, God was faithful. *I am here*, He whispered again.

To mark the moment, I took a picture. I had started to do that the previous summer and already had captured several rainbows on my phone. Each had shown up right as I needed it, and the record of each one, in all their bright colors and clear lines, brought me reassurance and joy every time I scrolled through the photos.

I looked at my phone to see the picture, since it was the most spectacular, vivid, and vibrant rainbow I had ever seen. It wasn't there. There were no colors, no lines, no rainbow at all. The picture was instead a bright white blaze of light that filled the entire screen.

A calm resolve and determination washed through me.

I looked at my sister in disbelief, and peace filled me. I spent the next two weeks back in Austin poring over tax code to make sure I personally understood what I was doing and the consequences. Monte brought the tax research into his firm—and in his generosity never charged me the $60,000 in billable hours he dedicated to finding answers.

Feeling only confirmation at every turn, and a peace and purpose I hadn't felt in months, I stiffened my spine and made the call one afternoon. "I'm paying everyone back. Now."

Two of my Three Wise Men and Jerry were not happy. My "best interests" were their main concerns, and protecting me was their top priority. My determination forced Monte and Jerry to write an official letter stating that I was acting contrary to their best legal advice. Even after presenting the letter to me, they knew I would not back down. Bill just laughed and accepted it. "She's going to do what she wants to do" had been his statement so often it didn't need repeating.

Here is my final communication on the subject, written September 4, 2014:

Monte & Bill,

I have finally made a decision and I have peace about it.

For the last two weeks I have had a very hard time knowing if I should pay the creditors now or in May. I didn't want to base my decision on what I selfishly wanted to do or on my emotions. I wanted my decision to be well thought out and rational so I knew I needed to seek wise counsel, that's y'all, to help advise me.

Over the past 15 months I have come to value your opinions so much I really wanted to know what you thought I should do. That is why it has been so important for me to know what you think, not only as my attorneys but as my friends as well. And not only what was the safest thing legally but what was the best thing for the creditors and my family.

I was really getting frustrated, not at y'all, but because I was not getting a clear answer. I wanted you all to agree on what to do and the fact that all of you didn't agree on what to do was very confusing for me. Then late yesterday afternoon it occurred to me that all of you (Bill, Monte, and Jeff) do agree on one thing and maybe that is the answer. You all agree that from a creditors' perspective it is best to pay them now.

So based on that and:

Philippians 2:3–4

³ Do nothing out of selfish ambition or vain conceit. Rather, in humility value others above yourselves, ⁴ not looking to your own interests but each of you to the interests of the others.

My decision is made. Pay the creditors now!

Wow, what a process to get to that point. Thank you very much for the hours and hours you have spent talking to me and helping me process everything.

I am so very thankful for you both and don't know what I would do without you.

Blessings,

Becky

PS: Just so there is no confusion I am fully aware this is NOT the SAFEST thing for me.

Here's Bill's ever-humorous reply:

I have been in a meeting.

Good call! Your three wise men and your team will back you up and will fight like hell to protect "the widow and the orphans." Be at peace, rest easy and let us do what we do. My loincloth is on (barely), the rag is tied around my head and the knife is between my teeth.

After laughing, and probably, crying, I replied:

Love you, Bill Jones.
   Thank you.
   Now get it done ASAP!!!!!

Chapter 12

Every storm runs, runs out of rain, just like every dark
night turns into day.

—"Every Storm Runs Out of Rain" by Gary Allan

It wasn't elation; it was purpose.

For the first time in seventeen months, I was moving
toward something, not just surviving something. But
surviving is not the same thing as thriving—and that's
what we want for our lives and for our children. This
was the first time I believed I was effecting change that
would rewrite our story for the better. That deep breath
I'd been wanting entered my lungs. From the very
beginning, I told my kids we would not be victims; now
I began to feel we could be more than survivors.

On September 17, Bill sent an email to the creditors
explaining the change in timing and our reasoning.
He also stated that the court-appointed trustee had to
be removed in favor of me returning as the estate's

trustee, so that I could take on the liability. If something went wrong, I would bear the consequences. With that change, Bill reassured the creditors that the estate remained under the jurisdiction of the Travis County Probate Court, and no money would pay out without its express approval.

On the afternoon the email went out, I was nervous—to the point of feeling sick. I wondered what the reaction might be, and I prayed everyone would trust us just a little longer. Melissa and I ran errands to distract me. She was driving down the street when a light outside the car window caught my eye. A gorgeous rainbow spanned the sky. I grabbed my phone, photographed it, and texted the picture to Monte and Bill: This is confirmation of my decision.

My lawyers got to work. We had started creating the settlement agreement in the fall the year before. We set to revising it. The agreement basically said, "I want to pay you back. You have to sign this and agree to not sue Invesco or me for more money in the future. You can't make any changes to this document as there are seventy-eight of you (not including Invesco and me), and we can't drag this out. Please sign within thirty days and I'll pay you 100 percent of your net loan to Mark." That's my version—the real document was thirty-four pages of legalese.

It was that legalese that took so long to create. A "global" settlement agreement not only meant that *everyone* needed to sign, but it had to cover *everything*.

It was an incredible document—both in its length and in its exhaustive nature. I wanted the agreement out on October 1; I wanted creditors to have two weeks to sign it; I wanted to be done with everything by Thanksgiving. As I told you, patience is not my strong suit.

Friends and I blew up the forty-foot Frosty in Monte's yard with a printed sign stating "October 1." I placed beneath the date two emojis, a high-heeled pink shoe and a gun. Ever since my "legal" document and receiving the shoes and the certificate, these emojis had become my signature for all texts and emails to my Three Wise Men. I wanted to add "Or Else" to the sign, but it sounded too ominous in my own mind. And my "Or Else" only meant I would keep adding Frosty's friends to Monte's yard every few nights until the agreement got out the door.

Monte knew instantly I was the author. But his neighbors did not. Even without the "Or Else," many found the sign, and especially the gun, frightening and called Monte concerned that he was in danger or being threatened.

The document was complex. It took time. October 1 came and went, and I did not add more inflatables to Monte's yard. The court approved the letter on October 13, and all copies were emailed and FedExed to the seventy-eight creditors within forty-eight hours.

I marked my calendar and started the thirty-day countdown. The October 13 start made the deadline to return the signed settlement agreement

November 14, 2014. Jerry made an appointment for a court hearing for that day, and we waited. The claims totaled $16,417,742.41, and the funds available, including the house and anything I had sold and the $5 million insurance policy once the creditor released his lien on it, totaled $17,204,866. After paying the creditors, I still had Mark's credit card debt to pay and other fees, and my own legal fees, but by my calculations when I included funds from the Atlantic Trust policy, it was going to work— almost to the penny.

Signed agreements came within hours. Jerry's assistant Kelly called or texted me as she received each one—she was as excited as I was. I soon added another calendar to my first. One marked days and one marked names. Within two weeks, we had seventy-two of the seventy-eight agreements back. I called Jerry to urge the last few creditors along.

We had all seventy-eight signatures back on October 31, two weeks before our hearing date. I didn't want to wait two days, much less two weeks. Jerry rushed to the courthouse and sat outside the judge's office in order to request an earlier hearing time. The judge was gracious, and we secured a time for November 10 at one-thirty p.m.

Monte sent an email to creditors stating that we expected judicial approval that day and that I would be in Monte's offices from eleven-thirty until two p.m. on November 11 to personally hand a check to anyone who was willing and able to come. He also assured them, "Don't worry if you can't come by during that time; Becky will mail all remaining checks that afternoon."

A personal delivery in this situation, as you can imagine, is not normal. Checks are sent FedEx, usually ten cents on the dollar, and all is done. But nothing was usual about this. It was a personal journey for my kids and me. I wanted to thank the creditors for waiting, thank them for trusting I would do the right thing and...I wanted a moment of closure with them, a moment to share my gratitude and the peace and joy I felt as the entire process came to a close.

I was so excited I asked Jerry if I could write out all the checks.

He stared at me. "You can't do that. They have to be cashier's checks."

"I want to sign them at least."

"You can't. The bank signs them."

That was Eddie Safady's job. On November 10, Monte let him know to get ready. We needed the $16.4 million in cashier's checks immediately upon receiving approval, since the next day was Veteran's Day and a bank holiday. Everyone knew I didn't want to wait for that, either. Eddie told us to hurry. He cautioned that it wasn't a simple process. Cutting that many checks, with all the paperwork required, would take hours.

Jerry, Bill, Johnny, Monte, and I stood before the judge and asked him to authorize payment to the creditors. He did. In hearing those words spoken, the lawyer for the creditor holding the lien on the $5 million policy also released that creditor's claim. We expected to celebrate right then and there, but we had to wait while the judge gave that lawyer an earful to pass on to his client—a reprimand for holding up the process and creating difficulties.

I fell into Bill's arms again, sobbing. He pulled out a hanky. In that gesture, I felt all the love and care I'd felt when my two friends gave me handkerchiefs soon after Mark's death. I hugged Bill again. He let me keep this handkerchief, too—now my collection is at three.

Johnny quipped, "I need to learn that trick."

We sent the paperwork to Eddie and grabbed a celebratory lunch; then the lawyers returned to their offices and I raced to the bank.

Three assistants helped Eddie, and within hours they had cut all the checks. Eddie handed the stack to me. I dropped them into a box and headed back downtown to Monte's office.

"I am so excited." I plopped down in a chair across from his desk and patted the box. "I have all the checks right here."

Monte's chair sprang forward so fast it almost propelled him across his desk. "You have over $16.4 million on your lap? In a shoebox?"

"But it's a Prada shoebox."

"Give me that." He snatched the box and placed it in his firm's safe.

That afternoon I went home and talked to John Luke.

He was floored. "Everybody everything?"

"Everybody everything," I confirmed.

"I thought you were going to spend the rest of your life paying everybody back, and I was going to help you when I got a job."

I hugged him tight. Each of my children had been so strong. And despite how often we shared and talked, they kept much of their pain and worry from me, just as I had worked to protect them.

Later that evening, I called Boone and Madison at Baylor. My older two had been privy to more details and fully understood what the next day meant for our family. I was reminded by the comments they made how much they had carried. I was so thankful a portion of their burden would be lifted.

I slept well that night.

And I got my wish—I would go into Christmas, my favorite time of the year, owing *no one* money.

Chapter 13

And I believe that everything in life is what it's meant
to be...I believe there's always hope when all
seems lost.

—"I Believe in Santa Claus" written by Dolly Parton,
and sung by Dolly Parton and Kenny Rogers

The next day, November 11, 2014, I stood in a conference room in Jackson Walker's Austin offices in a
khaki-colored dress and heels with that Prada shoebox
on the table in front of me. Before leaving Eddie at the
bank the day before, I had slid a printed note into each
envelope.

THERE ARE NO ADEQUATE WORDS TO DESCRIBE
HOW THANKFUL I AM FOR
YOUR KINDNESS, PATIENCE AND GRACE TO ME
AND MY CHILDREN THROUGH THIS
DIFFICULT TIME. I AM ETERNALLY GRATEFUL TO
EACH OF YOU. PLEASE KNOW
I PRAY GOD BLESSES YOU AND YOUR FAMILIES.

GRATEFULLY,

BECKY POWELL

"I THANK MY GOD EVERY TIME I REMEMBER YOU."
PHILIPPIANS 1:3

Jerry was shocked when he later learned about the notes. I hadn't asked permission because I had no idea I would need permission to thank someone. But I guess I did. Regardless, thirty creditors came that afternoon to pick up their checks, which meant I was able to personally thank thirty of them for their grace, patience, and trust. Several more called, disappointed they were unable to come personally. It seemed that everyone felt the excitement of this miracle. From day one, against all odds, nobody thought we'd be where we were.

And that's what Bill called it: a miracle. He still laughs that it happened at all. "That one person would behave like this and wait for you would be a miracle, but that over one hundred did is huge. A miracle beyond miracles."

One creditor asked why I "had gone beyond what you were called or required to do." I tried to explain that it wasn't beyond, but rather exactly what I was called and required to do. The last creditor to pick up his check that afternoon was John Needham, the creditor who had sent the compassionate note to Bill after the first creditors' meeting a year earlier. We talked for a while, and then he stayed a few minutes and asked if he could pray with me. With tears in my eyes, I said yes.

Once again, God showed up.

Later that evening, another creditor called me to say that as she rode the elevator down after receiving her check, the man next to her stated, "I drove from Houston just to meet her. I've never seen anybody do what she did." I cried at hearing that—for that was what had surprised me the most. I was so grateful that the creditors felt as blessed by the day as I had been. But the idea that they were coming to show me their gratitude was surprising; it shouldn't have been. After all, that's what I'd witnessed the entire time—an extraordinary measure of grace. To hear it articulated that afternoon by so many people felt wonderful and confirming.

The next day, Johnny called Alan Buie, the Assistant United States Attorney, to tell him all creditors had been paid.

Johnny then called me. "Right there, on the phone, the AUSA declared the DOJ would close the case. He said that never in all his years has he seen everyone get paid back in full in this kind of situation, and he asked me to tell you how impressed they are by you, and they are very sorry for your loss...Congratulations, Becky. I'm so happy for you."

Jerry contacted the SEC to let them know the same thing. After he hung up with them, he emailed me: She was very pleased. Becky, she had high praise for you.

But it wasn't just me...I was one set of hands and

feet. God guided the miracle. He guided it through me and through the hearts of more than one hundred good people. As Bill said, more than one hundred people had to participate—and did. We needed seventy-eight to wait patiently, then sign the settlement agreement. We needed the thirteen Atlantic Trust clients to cooperate with Invesco; and then you add my attorneys, the thirty-six creditor attorneys, plus all the Invesco attorneys. You soon have well over one hundred people! Friends told me that one creditor, amazed by all that had happened, turned around and gave his $125,000 repayment to charity within days of receiving his check.

November 14, the original due date for the settlement agreements, was the only date my lawyers were available to celebrate. A few could not make it, but my four main attorneys had marked this date on their calendars, and I couldn't let it go to waste. Stephen Shallcross, owner of 2 Dine 4, who had catered our Christmas parties and supplied the box lunches for the gathering at Mark's graveside, offered his catering house, Swoop House, for a special dinner.

I blew up Frosty in front of the building and my Three Wise Men (Bill, Monte, and Johnny), Jerry and I, and all their wives, gathered inside to celebrate the end of a long journey. In the days between November 11 and 14, I had paid Mark's credit card debt and my remaining debts and fees. I had also tithed 10 percent of what remained. It was imperative to give back to God in this way. I also used part of that money to honor my main attorneys.

For Bill and Monte, who had both attended Baylor Law School, I created a scholarship in their name—to raise up future lawyers with their integrity and caliber.

For Johnny, I asked a friend of mine who is an accomplished jewelry designer and silversmith to craft a belt buckle with his initials on it.

And for Jerry, I purchased five Hermès ties. Mark used to wear beautiful Hermès ties, and the first time I met Jerry he was wearing one, too. That was another moment for me when God said, *I am here*, as Jerry's tie alone had made me feel instantly comfortable. Not only that, but I'd also found a special one.

One afternoon during a meeting, Jerry sat back in his chair dumbfounded by my optimism and trust that God would see us through the morass. Jerry shook his head and looked to Bill. "Where does she get her juju?"

Bill laughed and shot back, "You know perfectly well where she gets her juju."

I had been very open about my faith and beliefs for eighteen months. As I handed him an Hermès tie covered in fishes that night, I told him that they looked like the Christian ichthus symbol. "This is to always remind you where I get my juju."

He called one day, weeks later, laughing. "I had a tough case today and wore the tie. I won!"

That night was full of joy, friendship, laughing, and a profound sense of relief and gratitude. I was beyond elated to enter into the Christmas season owing no one money. I could finally enjoy the season and was excited to create new memories.

A group of my friends hold a White Elephant Christmas Party each year. In early December, Corey Ray sent out an email with the challenge to create a poem for the party with a prize for the winner. My mind immediately turned to Ecclesiastes, and my entry summed up my journey:

There is an appointed time for everything under
   the sun.
A time to steal a car and a time to decal one.
A time to be invited to the Rays and go and a time
   to be invited to David Wise's and not.
A time to have wine and a time to have hot tea.
A time to go to Uchi with your husband and a time
   to get your ass there without him.
A time to cry and a time to cry.
A time to drink red wine and a time to spill it on a
   really nice sofa.
A time to read the *Austin American-Statesman* and
   a time to burn it.
A time to have no attorneys and a time to have eight.
A time to wear underwear and a time to forget.
A time to call someone "liar liar pants on fire" and
   a time not to call your criminal attorney one.

A time to know *of* the FBI, SEC, DOJ and IRS and
a time to be known *by* them.
A time to have sex and a time to be a born-again
virgin.
A time to be a friend and a time to need a friend.
There is nothing new under the sun.

I won!

Most of the poem's references I've mentioned within these pages. I'll call out a few I haven't directly talked about. I often found in social situations, when others were drinking, that it felt good to have something in my hand. Often it was a cup of hot tea. The heat soothed me just as having the cup in my hand felt socially appropriate. As for the red wine across the sofa...Chrissy Ray is a neat freak, and that's an understatement. At our group's 2013 party, we were passing around a chipped red wineglass (the coveted white elephant gift that year) and I turned it over to look at the chip. Because the glass was red, I had no idea it was full of wine. The wine poured all over me, Chrissy's $6,000 sofa, and her even more expensive rug. The entire party froze, and all eyes shot to Chrissy, expecting an explosion. It was a growth moment for her—she started laughing. Friends say that wouldn't have been her reaction if anyone else had done that or if my husband hadn't died months before, but I like to believe she's loosening up.

At another Christmas party a few days later (we're back to 2014 now), a friend walked up to me and said, "Oh, my gosh, look at Leslie's blouse. It has gems bedazzled on it, and I thought it was a real diamond necklace. You should tell her you like it."

The two of us walked over to Leslie, to whom I had repaid almost one million dollars two weeks before. I smiled and gestured to her blouse. "I love your necklace."

Leslie didn't miss a beat. She brought a hand up to her neck and stroked the appliquéd gems. "Thank you. I recently came into some money."

Our poor friend paled in horror, but Leslie and I roared with laughter.

Life was getting back to normal.

Chapter 14

I love this crazy, tragic, sometimes almost magic, awful,
beautiful life.

—"Awful Beautiful Life" by Darryl Worley

Almost seven years have passed since Mark died. I've
learned much and changed much during that time. The
Global Settlement Agreement put into writing that I
fully absorbed the cost of Mark's actions. The IRS has
never pursued the case nor contacted any of the creditors. Precedent states that the IRS takes a backseat
to creditors being made whole in such situations, and
we rely on that. Representatives from the SEC and
DOJ also gave us their stamps of approval. They were
shocked by the outcome and believed it ended far
better than ever expected—900 percent better to be
exact, considering the "good outcome" of ten cents on
the dollar. In effect, it feels as if any and all questions
are behind us.

Well, not all questions…I am still asked today, "Aren't you mad?"

The answer is no. I chose to marry Mark and all that came with that. And even if I had never expected this chapter in my life, I believed then what I continue to believe now: Had God wanted any aspect of it to be different, it would have been different. Rather than wishing I could have avoided or skipped this moment of our lives, I am so grateful God chose to be present within it. Yes, if I had my choice, Mark would be beside me. He is not. Yet God has proven Himself faithful, and I hand Him that lost desire too.

The Corinthians verse I inscribed in Mark's wedding ring—*Love is patient, love is kind. It does not envy, it does not boast, it is not proud.* (1 Corinthians 13:4)—is often read at weddings. But it's not about marriage. It's about life. It's how we are called to live, to love, and to share in each other's hopes and hurts.

In that vein, I still love Mark, and I still hurt for him. My heart continues to ache for all Mark went through and did; it aches for his friends who felt betrayed; and it aches for my children. My heart also aches that my husband died thinking he had taken care of us with his insurance money, and that played a role in his motivation for leaving us.

My story is well known in Austin, but not so much outside our community. It should have been. Countless times it could have gotten out and been made larger, but it didn't. Although we certainly felt the pressure of the media, it was so much better than it could or even should have been. It was in that relatively quiet space that all this happened. I do believe that had our story been canvassed in the media more fully, many creditors might have gotten anxious and filed suit against me. It would have become the "bloodbath" Bill Jones antici-pated. Instead, it was as far from that as it could be. It was hard, and more than one hundred people had to co-operate. But the absence of all that was normal allowed for the extraordinary.

That extraordinary continues to bless our lives.

Madison was at a political fund-raiser for her em-ployer one evening when Admiral Robert R. Inman approached her. His generous comments in an early *Austin American-Statesman* article I believe helped set the tone in those first days. He had said, "That's the nature of the business, you're fortunate if one in three (deals) are successful." He then expressed concern over my kids and my welfare, hoping we were "taken care of before the investors get paid."

That evening, he and his wife hugged Madison and told her they had never seen or heard of anyone do what our family did, and that she should be proud.

Madison called me immediately. "Why didn't you tell me we owed them money?"

I could only shake my head. "I didn't know if I should."

It's hard even today to know what to tell and what to keep silent. That night, I hung up the phone and cried...Yes, I still cry a lot, but for different reasons now. Our family has a new story. Madison was not met with stares or condemnation or even questions. She was met with love. That's one thing I hope all the creditors, the lawyers, the government agencies, and the judges who were part of our journey understand—without the respect, care, generosity, and patience they showed us, we would not be where we are today. Madison could have had a very different conversation and we could all carry a very different story. I am beyond thankful for the story we've been given.

Once I was given permission to find work, I had given thought to open an event planning business and created an LLC for the venture: 2CW for Two Cents Worth. I named it after the Widow's Offering from Mark 12:42–44: *But a poor widow came and put in two very small copper coins, worth only a few cents. Calling his disciples to him, Jesus said, "Truly I tell you, this poor widow has put more into the treasury than all the others. They all gave out of their wealth; but she, out of her poverty, put in everything—all she had to live on."*

These verses meant a great deal to me during those eighteen months. Each day I had to be willing to put in my last two cents, no matter what was left. In the end, all my expenses were covered. I had enough to pay the creditors, Mark's credit card debt, and my legal expenses, all of which totaled more than $19 million. On that note, I believe, my legal expenses should have been closer to $5 million. But because my attorneys purposely failed to bill me for all of their hours and so many creditors and their lawyers cooperated, I paid only $1.7 million.

As I said, I then tithed what remained. I continue to do that with any money I make, and will do so with anything I earn from this book as well. From my earnings from *Awful Beautiful Life*, my tithe will be divided between the Helping Hand Home and Young Life, two organizations I remain passionate about. I am not faithful in this way to win God's favor, but faithful in gratitude for His continued generosity and love toward me.

I am now an insurance agent. Thanks to Monte I decided not to pursue the event-planning business. Starting a new business takes capital, capital I don't have. But it also takes, as Monte reminded me, "charging your friends full price for your business help." While I might be willing to give my "two cents' worth" in opinions, both Monte and I suspected I'd have a hard time charging full price for it.

I spent late 2014 and early 2015 studying for my insurance licensing exams, and I thoroughly enjoy my work. It's hard, which I like, and it has allowed me the flexibility to see John Luke through high school. He headed to college this fall, and Madison and Boone have long graduated from Baylor and both returned to Austin. The kids and I are closer than ever, sharing meals each week, since I will never be above the bribery of offering free food. And yes, as Kate promised so long ago, I am learning to trust again.

I have also learned in the past seven years of the burden of guilt many carried and still carry over Mark's debt and death. Many creditors sensed something wrong in Mark's stories, but they were his friends—and we want to believe the best of our friends. After his death, many felt that if they had come to Mark with their suspicions they could have prevented his death. Before the entire story came out in those early days, one creditor even called my lawyers, certain that his loan to Mark had been the only one and therefore was the reason for Mark's suicide.

Others felt guilt that they had never suspected anything was wrong. I carried that guilt for a long time, too. I was married to Mark for more than twenty-two years, and for all that time, he lied to me—and I never suspected a thing. *Was I not looking? Was I self-absorbed? Did I enjoy what we had too much to question it?* I could go crazy with all the questions, as have a couple of my dear friends. None of the questions, however, will help any of us take our next steps. God has helped me surrender all this to Him, and my hope is that every creditor involved will lay it down as well.

That said, I have heard that a few creditors have created rules for either loaning money to friends or for entering into investment opportunities. A few talk to each other in the form of an accountability group. A few have said they will never lend money unless the recipient's spouse is fully aware. And a few said they will never lend or invest with friends again. Period.

Learning that tidbit alone shows that, despite how much is within these pages, there is so much that is missing as well. Mark's death and his financial scandal touched many lives.

Seven years later, God has healed me from some of the most raw and painful moments. Some I have forgotten. Some I see and feel in a more forgiving light. That's part of the story, too. God showed up again and again, saying each time: *I am here.* He has proved faithful.

Near the end of this journey, I was given one of my favorite verses: *He has shown you, O mortal, what is good. And what does the Lord require of you? To act justly and to love mercy and to walk humbly with your God* (Micah 6:8).

Walking, stepping forward every day in faith, is the call He has laid upon my heart.

He has also laid another call upon heart. Matthew 6:20 encourages us to *store up for yourselves treasures in heaven, where moths and vermin do not destroy, and where thieves do not break in and steal.* We had so many "treasures" before Mark died. And, as Kristian Bush reminds us in "Trailer Hitch," "We've never seen a hearse with a trailer hitch." We can't take stuff with us when we die.

I don't miss all those "treasures" and all that stuff. I feel blessed beyond belief with the friendship, faith, fun, and family—four of the pillars I alluded to earlier—that God has lavished on us. I hope that my kids and I will always remember and share what we've learned. I hope we will walk with friends through tragedy and, as Madison said, "just show up." Those are the treasures that moths and thieves cannot destroy and that God through time will only burnish brighter.

Epilogue

Awful Beautiful Life came from God's hands as well. Friends continually asked me to write my story. I would reply each and every time, "If God wants the story told, He'll bring me a writer." He did. A mutual friend, in an extraordinary way, connected Katherine and me. We had been acquaintances years before when Katherine lived in Austin and John Luke was in kindergarten with her daughter, but we hadn't kept in touch. In fact, before my close friend Suzanne called her, she hadn't heard about my story at all. Yet we felt like old friends in our first conversation, which by the way was on May 16, 2016. After months of seeking a mutually agreeable time to talk, the anniversary of Mark's death was the only available date. At the end of our long talk, I told her that fact, and the line went silent for a moment. She then commented, "I can't believe I'm saying this, but I think I'm supposed to write your story." So we began...

On a final note, on May 8, 2015—the original pay-out date according to the IRS paperwork we filed—I received an IRS refund check from my 2014 taxes. It had nothing to do with all of this, but it came on that very day, and it made me laugh. I took a picture of it to dinner that night to show my attorneys since we'd had this special date on our books for months.

We gathered at Congress, David Bull's sister restaurant to Second Kitchen. And, as a gift-giver, I had a gift for each of them. I had acquired ancient coins, widow's mites, and I placed two in each of four clear plastic coin sleeves. On the outside, I had printed "May 8, 2015." As I had given all I had, so had my lawyers.

They had a gift for me, too. They had each saved the gift cards for Second Kitchen I'd given them on November 14 the year before, and they used them to pay for the dinner.

While my Three Wise Men and Jerry remain important men in my life, dinner that evening marked the end of this journey together. They are no longer on my payroll!

<hr />

Let your light shine before others, that they may see your good deeds and glorify your Father in heaven (Matthew 5:16). This verse has become true in my life, as you'll see in the following letters, that glorify God even as they honor me. To God be the glory!

Kerry N. Cammack

919 Congress Avenue, Suite 1400
Austin, Texas 78701

November 14, 2014

Mrs. Becky Powell
1036 Liberty Park Drive, Unit 36
Austin, TX 78746

Dear Becky:

It was really great to visit with you, if even briefly, on election night with Michael and Linda McCaul. It has been a real joy to see Michael progress up the ranks in leadership in Congress, now chairing a very important committee.

As I had mentioned in my letter to you shortly after Mark's tragic death, I cannot image the pain and heartache that you were going through then, and have gone through in the months since.

A tragic death is always a sad event, but even more so when the death is so senseless as was Mark's.

The courage you have shown and the great integrity in the manner by which you have dealt with the financial challenges confronting Mark's estate is one of the most admirable things I have ever observed in my life. Your tenacity and intense desire to do the right thing teaches all of us many lessons about decency and honor that I think many would not have shown if placed in your circumstances.

I appreciate very much personally your diligent efforts to obtain recovery of the funding that was made to Mark and I hope that your circumstances are such that you will be able to live life to the fullest going forward.

I wish you and all of your children my very best and am hopeful our paths will cross again in the very near future. In fact, I am hopeful that during the holidays, we can all get together, perhaps with the McCauls, to enjoy the season and to celebrate the beginning of a new year.

Again, thanks for being such an outstanding person. I look forward to seeing you soon.

Cordially,

All The best Becky!!

Kerry N. Cammack

Walter A. DeRoeck
1801 Lavaca Street, Suite 109
Austin, Texas 78701
(512) 422-3738

November 11, 2014

Ms. Becky Powell
1036 Liberty Park Drive #36
Austin, Texas 78746

Dear Becky,

I wanted to write you a letter hoping not only you would read it, but your children, too. I was president of a bank for 19 years, and during that time I faced many unpleasant situations where people dismissed their obligations. Occasionally some memorable family stepped forward and paid their debt. That, however, occurred very rarely. Looking back over those years, I cannot compare what you have done to any of those other experiences. You have given up your financial security, the equity in your home, reduced your standard of living, and subjected your children to the same fate. You made these sacrifices even though you did not have to do so legally. In short, you are unique, and words are inadequate to express my admiration and respect.

In the nearly 25 years I have known you, I would never have assumed that you would be the person who would impact my life in such a meaningful way. I hope your children recognize that their mother is extraordinary. Not only does she talk the talk, but walks the walk when it comes to character, respect, and doing the right thing.

Forever your admirer and friend,

Wally

Becky,

Mere words cannot express the respect and adoration that I have for you. You were dealt an unbelievable set of circumstances and you persevered and triumphed over it all. Becky, you are an amazing person and Leslie & I are fortunate to be your friend. We love you. May God bless you.

Tim

Frank P. Krasovec • Chairman

November 11, 2014

Becky Powell
c/o Jerry Frank Jones
400 W. 15th St., Suite 975
Austin, TX 78701

Dear Becky:

Thank you for having the courage and character to "do what was right". Lessons in life are not easy to teach but you have set a great example for your family and many others.

I am in Dallas today working with my son Mark. Your actions will be communicated as an example of maintaining strong values in times of adversity.

If I can ever be of assistance to you or your family, I would welcome a call from you.

Thank you.

Frank P. Krasovec

FPK/cjs

11/20/14

Ms. Rebecca Powell,

Dear Ms. Powell,

I want to express my condolences to you for the loss of your husband and the difficulties encountered by your family. I can scarcely imagine what heartaches and strains this situation has imposed upon you.

The way you have handled this extremely difficult situation not only does credit to your character, but even more importantly bestows a priceless legacy of integrity on your children. I wish you a holiday season of peace, and happiness in the years to come.

Kind regards,
Steve Fleckman

If you'd like to read the entire agreement I wrote to my Three Wise Men, I include it here. Writing it allowed me to reframe many of the serious issues surrounding me in a humorous light. And I had a tremendous amount of fun doing it, and gained a wonderful pair of pink shoes!

Agreement and Consent
Regarding Compliance with Legal Advice

This **Agreement and Consent Regarding Compliance with Legal Advice** (the "*Agreement*") is made and entered into as of this February 9, 2014 by and between Bill Jones, an individual resident of Travis County, Texas ("Jones"), Monte James, an individual resident of Travis County, Texas ("James"), Johnny Sutton, an individual resident of Travis County, Texas ("Sutton"), and together with Jones and James, collectively referred to herein as "The Three Wise Men," and Rebecca Lee Powell, an individual resident of Travis County, Texas [and financial supporter of The Three Wise Men] ("Powell").

Recitals:

WHEREAS, Powell hired The Three Wise Men, as well as a legion of other attorneys, to represent her as legal counsel in the midst of numerous investigations;

WHEREAS, Powell specifically hired The Wise Men not only because of their good looks but their legal expertise and sheer brilliance, but because as Powell's client, they pledged to represent her in accordance with her judgment and wishes;

WHEREAS, recent events have caused Powell continuous and significant mental and emotional anguish and distress;

WHEREAS, despite the fact that The Three Wise Men have pledged to represent her in accordance with her judgment and wishes, The Three Wise Men have materially contributed to the aforesaid continuous and significant mental and emotional anguish and distress by all but coercing her to follow certain legal advice, against her vehement protests, which is certain to cause Powell continued significant mental and emotional anguish and distress;

WHEREAS, because Powell is attempting to trust The Three Wise Men, Powell is unwillingly consenting to follow The Three Wise Men's legal advice with respect to these matters;

WHEREAS, in consideration of Powell consenting to follow The Three Wise Men's legal advice with respect to these matters, Powell is conditioning her consent on certain stipulations to be strictly complied with by The Three Wise Men, as further set forth herein;

Agreement:

NOW, THEREFORE, in consideration of the mutual premises and consideration and other good and valuable consideration, the receipt and sufficiency of which are hereby acknowledged, The Three Wise Men and Powell, intending to be legally bound, hereby agree as follows:

1. The Recitals set forth above are hereby incorporated in their totality into this Agreement.

2. Subject to The Three Wise Men's strict compliance with Section 3 below, Powell hereby consents to abide by The Three Wise Men's legal counsel with respect to waiting until May 8, 2015, to pay back creditors according to the expiration of the IRS statute of limitations of whatever the heck it's called.

3. In consideration for Powell's consent described in Section 2, The Three Wise Men agree as follows:

a. In the event that The Three Wise Men's advice causes Powell to experience further significant mental and emotional anguish and distress (which advice is against Powell's wishes and vast legal wisdom and which Powell has previously made clear she does not want to follow), each of the following shall be promptly fulfilled to, in part, compensate Powell for such additional mental and emotional anguish and distress which none of The Three Wise Men can fully appreciate:

i. Jones shall purchase, because of his impeccable taste in women's footwear, for Powell footwear of his choice (which footwear must be acceptable to Powell, in her *sole* discretion, without regard to price, style, color, design, or otherwise, and without regard to whether such footwear consists of heels, boots, sandals, slippers, wooden clogs, or any other footwear of whatever kind with the exception of athletic footwear), when she feels like it, in perpetuity, or until such mental and emotional anguish and distress drives Powell to her grave.

ii. James shall purchase for Powell one firearm of his choice (which firearm must be acceptable to Powell, in her discretion, without regard to price, style, color, design, or otherwise, and without regard to whether such firearm is a pistol, handgun, shotgun, assault rifle, or otherwise), on an annual basis, in perpetuity, or until such mental and emotional anguish and distress drives Powell to her grave. Please note, Powell promises not to shoot The Three Wise Men with said firearms.

iii. Sutton shall provide Powell and each of her children a "Get Out of Jail Free" card in perpetuity for any and all future criminal acts that Powell is driven to commit as a result of such additional mental and emotional anguish and distress that she is forced to endure during such additional fifteen (15) month period, as well as all crimes that each of her children may be compelled to commit as a result of Powell's mental and emotional anguish and distress. Such full legal representation shall also include full legal representation with respect to any commitment proceedings initiated by the State of Texas's Office of Mental Health and Rehabilitation, and any medical costs incurred as a result of any such commitment.

iv. The Three Wise Men are responsible to fully remit to the appropriate taxing authority all taxes owed by Powell (including any and all personal, business, and investment income, ad valorem, personal, estate, and gift taxes now and hereafter due) in perpetuity. It hereby being stipulated by Powell that she currently is unemployed.

v. The Three Wise Men shall, jointly and severally, also provide Powell with the following as partial compensation for Powell's added mental and emotional anguish and distress:

b. In the event that during such 15 month period, as a result of The Three Wise Men's advice any such creditor of Powell (and or, as applicable, [the Powell Estate]) causes any (even in the slightest way) additional emotional distress, as determined by Powell in her discretion, The Three Wise Men shall:

i. Provide her with sweets (no chocolate, please).

c. In the event that during such 15 month

period, as a result of Becky's Attorney's advice article regarding Powell (and or, as applicable, [the Powell Estate]) is caused to be published in any newspaper or periodical of general circulation, or any electronic or "blog" website which causes any (even in the slightest way) additional emotional distress, as determined by Powell in her discretion, The Three Wise Men shall:

i. Provide her with spa or beach days at the location of her choice based on the content of any such publication. In some cases, this may require her leaving the country to get away from the media attention causing the distress.

4. All of the obligations of The Three Wise Men as described in Section 3 herein (except for Section 3(a)(i) which obligation is the sole responsibility of Jones) are joint and several obligations of each of The Three Wise Men. Each such obligation shall be fulfilled exclusively by The Three Wise Men and shall not be fulfilled or aided, in any way, by any other person (including the spouses of The Three Wise Men). However, in the case of Section 3(c)(i) resulting in her having to leave the country it would be necessary to be accompanied by Johnita Jones and Katherine James and my special legal counsel Mary Beth Arcidiacono.

5. In the unlikely event that, upon the expiration of such 15-month period, The Three Wise Men's legal counsel results in a favorable outcome,

(whereas Powell was wrong) in such event, Powell hereby agrees to:

a. Throw a big party for The Three Wise Men and admit she was wrong once a year for life.

6. By signing this Agreement, each of The Three Wise Men hereby represents and warrants to Powell that they are guaranteeing that such legal counsel will result in the best possible outcome to Powell and they fully understand Powell's objections and warrant that they fully anticipate that there shall be no negative consequences, mental, emotional, legal, or otherwise to Powell as a result of her consent to follow such legal counsel.

7. Each of THE THREE WISE MEN, jointly and severally, hereby agree to fully indemnify and hold Powell harmless from any such negative consequences, which shall be determined in Powell's sole discretion, that may result from acquiescing to follow such legal advice. Each hereby agrees to fully represent Powell, at no cost to Powell, for any such legal costs and expenses which arise therefrom in response to any claims related thereto, including, but not limited to, any mental health bills (including massages and vacations) of any kind. Such indemnity shall survive the expiration or earlier termination of this Agreement.

8. **Under no circumstance whatsoever ARE GUNS AND SHOES SUBJECT TO CLAW-BACK.**

9. The parties to this Agreement each mutually agree that upon the execution hereof by each of the parties hereto, this Agreement shall be fully binding and effective as to each party and shall not be subject to approval by any person or authority, **including Judge Herman, IRS, SEC, DOJ, or FBI.**

10. This Agreement may be executed in one or more counterparts, each of which shall constitute an original.

11. This Agreement shall be binding upon and inure to the benefit of and be enforceable by the parties hereto, particularly Powell, and their respective successors, assigns, including any spouses, heirs, and personal and legal representatives. The Three Wise Men shall require and cause any successor (whether direct or indirect by purchase, merger, consolidation or otherwise) to all, substantially all, or a substantial part, of the business and/or assets of each of The Three Wise Men respective employers, by written agreement in form and substance satisfactory to Powell, expressly to assume and agree to perform this Agreement in the same manner and to the same extent that The Three Wise Men would be required to perform if no such succession had taken place.

12. The parties hereto hereby represent that they have each had the opportunity to have their individual legal counsel review this Agreement and that

they desire to enter into this Agreement of their own accord.

13. Any inquiries related to the interpretation of this Agreement shall be arbitrated by Powell's special counsel, Mary Beth Lee Arcidiacono ("Arcidiacono"). Arcidiacono shall have exclusive jurisdiction over the interpretation of the provisions hereof, and except as specifically set forth herein, sole discretion to determine whether any party hereto has adequately performed their respective obligations hereunder. The parties hereby unequivocally consent to such jurisdiction and hereby agree to Arcidiacono's decision as to any matter related hereto is final and unappealable to any tribunal of any jurisdiction. Special counsel Arcidiacono may require shoe and travel support (you can keep your guns) from The Wise Men as payment for having to deal with Ms. Powell (Little Miss Can't Be Wrong) the past 46 years.

14. This Agreement sets forth the entire understanding between the parties hereto and supersedes and merges all previous written and oral negotiations, commitments, understandings and agreements relating to the subject matter hereof between the parties hereto.

IN WITNESS WHEREOF, the parties hereto have executed this Indemnification Agreement on and as of the day and year first above written.

REBECCA LEE POWELL

_____

BILL JONES

_____

MONTE JAMES

_____

JOHNNY SUTTON

_____

ACKNOWLEDGED AND AGREED:

MARY BETH LEE ARCIDIACONO

_____

I cannot say enough how much country music lifted me during this time. I wanted to include my top 500 songs, but that's too many; and I couldn't narrow it down to 100. So here are my top 200 favorite country songs, just in case you too need a little hope to lift your heartbreak.

"All I Ask for Anymore"—Trace Adkins
"All My Ex's Live in Texas"—George Strait
"All Over Me"—Josh Turner
"All the Gold in California"—Larry Gatlin & the Gatlin Brothers
"All the Rage in Paris"—The Derailers
"Always on My Mind"—Willie Nelson
"Amen Kind of Love"—Daryle Singletary
"Another Side of You"—Joe Nichols
"Anyway"—Martina McBride
"As Good As I Once Was"—Toby Keith
"As She's Walking Away"—Zac Brown Band
"Awful Beautiful Life"—Darryl Worley
"Back at One"—Mark Wills
"Baggage Claim"—Miranda Lambert
"Bar Exam"—The Derailers
"Barbed Wire Halo"—Aaron Watson
"Barefoot and Crazy"—Jack Ingram
"Bartender"—Lady Antebellum
"Beer for My Horses"—Toby Keith and Willie Nelson
"Before He Cheats"—Carrie Underwood
"A Better Man"—Clint Black
"Bless the Broken Road"—Rascal Flatts

"Blessed"—Martina McBride

"Boot Scootin' Boogie"—Brooks & Dunn

"Bring It On Home"—Little Big Town

"Broken Halos"—Chris Stapleton

"Broken Lady"—Larry Gatlin & the Gatlin Brothers

"Can't Get Away from a Good Time"—Logan Mize

"Carolina in the Pines"—Michael Martin Murphey

"Carried Away"—George Strait

"Celebrity"—Brad Paisley

"Cleaning This Gun"—Rodney Atkins

"Come a Little Closer"—Dierks Bentley

"Complicated"—Carolyn Dawn Johnson

"Die a Happy Man"—Thomas Rhett

"Do You Believe Me Now"—Jimmy Wayne

"Do You Wanna Go to Heaven"—T. G. Sheppard

"Don't It Make My Brown Eyes Blue"—Crystal Gayle

"Don't Ya"—Brett Eldredge

"Downtown"—Lady Antebellum

"Drink, Swear, Steal & Lie"—Michael Peterson

"Drunk on a Plane"—Dierks Bentley

"Emotional Girl"—Terri Clark

"Every Storm (Runs Out of Rain)"—Gary Allan

"Fast As You"—Dwight Yoakam

"Feels Like Love"—Vince Gill

"Feels So Right"—Alabama

"Fight Like a Girl"—Kalie Shorr

"Find Out Who Your Friends Are"—Tracy Lawrence

"Firecracker"—Josh Turner

"The Fireman"—George Strait

"Fly"—Maddie & Tae

"Forever and Ever, Amen"—Randy Travis

"Forever Country"—Artists of Then, Now & Forever

"Gettin' You Home"—Chris Young

"Girl in a Country Song"—Maddie & Tae

"Girls in Bikinis"—Lee Brice

"Give It Away"—George Strait

"God Bless the U.S.A."—Lee Greenwood

"God Gave Me You"—Blake Shelton

"God, Your Mama, and Me"— Florida Georgia Line (feat.
    Backstreet Boys)

"Good Hearted Woman"—Waylon Jennings & Willie
    Nelson

"H.O.L.Y."—Florida Georgia Line

"Harper Valley P.T.A."—Jeannie C. Riley

"He Didn't Have to Be"—Brad Paisley

"Head Over Boots"—Jon Pardi

"High Maintenance Woman"—Toby Keith

"Hold On to Me"—John Michael Montgomery

"Holding Her and Loving You"—Earl Thomas Conley

"Home Alone Tonight"—Luke Bryan (feat. Karen
    Fairchild)

"Home to You"—John Michael Montgomery

"Honey Bee"—Blake Shelton

"Hope You Get Lonely Tonight"—Cole Swindell

"How Do You Like Me Now?!"—Toby Keith

"Humble and Kind"—Tim McGraw

"I Believe in You"—Don Williams

"I Don't Dance"—Lee Brice

"I Found Jesus on the Jailhouse Floor"—George Strait

"I Got a Feelin'"—Billy Currington

"I Have to Surrender"—Ty Herndon

"I Left Something Turned On at Home"—Trace Adkins

"I Love a Rainy Night"—Eddie Rabbitt

"I Met a Girl"—Eddie Rabbitt

"I Swear"—John Michael Montgomery

"I Told You So"—Carrie Underwood (feat. Randy Travis)

"I Walk the Line"—Johnny Cash

"I Wanna Talk about Me"—Toby Keith

"I Was Country When Country Wasn't Cool"
    —Barbara Mandrell and George Jones

"I Won't Take Less Than Your Love"—Tanya Tucker

"I'm Gonna Hire a Wino to Decorate Our Home"
    —David Frizzell

"If I Never Stop Loving You"—David Kersh

"If I Said You Had a Beautiful Body Would You Hold It
    Against Me"—The Bellamy Brothers

"If You're Going Through Hell (Before the Devil Even
    Knows)"—Rodney Atkins

"If You're Gonna Play in Texas (You Gotta Have a Fiddle
    in the Band)"—Alabama

"I'll Walk"—Bucky Covington

"I'm Movin' On"—Rascal Flatts

"I'm Not Strong Enough to Say No"—BlackHawk

"I'm Still a Guy"—Brad Paisley

"In Case You Didn't Know"—Brett Young

"It's Five O'Clock Somewhere"—Alan Jackson and
    Jimmy Buffett

"It's Hard to Kiss the Lips at Night That Chew Your Ass
    Out All Day Long"—The Notorious Cherry Bombs

"Jesus, Take the Wheel"—Carrie Underwood

"John Deere Green"—Joe Diffie

"Just Got Started Lovin' You"—James Otto

"Just to See You Smile"—Tim McGraw

"Keep Me in Mind"—Zac Brown Band

"The Keeper of the Stars"—Tracy Byrd

"Kiss an Angel Good Morning"—Charley Pride

"Later On"—The Swon Brothers

"Let Your Love Flow"—Bellamy Brothers

"A Little Bit Stronger"—Sara Evans

"Lonely Tonight"—Blake Shelton (feat. Ashley Monroe)

"Look It Up"—Ashton Shepherd

"Lookin' for Love"—Johnny Lee

"Lord, I Hope This Day Is Good"—Don Williams

"Lose My Mind"—Brett Eldredge

"Love in the First Degree"—Alabama

"Loved Too Much"—Ty Herndon

"Loving You Easy"—Zac Brown Band

"Makin' This Boy Go Crazy"—Dylan Scott

"Mama's Broken Heart"—Miranda Lambert

"The Man I Want to Be"—Chris Young

"Me and God"—Josh Turner

"Mean to Me"—Brett Eldredge

"Mine Would Be You"—Blake Shelton

"Must Be Doin' Somethin' Right"—Billy Currington

"My Eyes"—Blake Shelton (feat. Gwen Sebastian)

"Nobody"—Sylvia

"Nobody to Blame"—Chris Stapleton

"Oh, Pretty Woman"—Roy Orbison

"Old Alabama"—Brad Paisley (feat. Alabama)

"Old Flame"—Alabama

"Old Man Walker's Property"—Aaron Watson

"On the Other Hand"—Randy Travis

"One Night at a Time"—George Strait

"Outskirts of Heaven"—Craig Campbell

"People Are Crazy"—Billy Currington

"Perfect Storm"—Brad Paisley

"Pray for You"—Jaron and the Long Road to Love

"Rain Is a Good Thing"—Luke Bryan

"Remind Me"—Carrie Underwood (duet
    with Brad Paisley)

"The Rest of Mine"—Trace Adkins

"Rhinestone Cowboy"—Glen Campbell

"Riser"—Dierks Bentley

"She Don't Tell Me To"—Montgomery Gentry

"She Keeps the Home Fires Burning"—Ronnie Milsap

"She Let Herself Go"—George Strait

"Shotgun Rider"—Tim McGraw

"Slow Hand"—Conway Twitty

"Smoky Mountain Rain"—Ronnie Milsap

"Some Beach"—Blake Shelton

"Somebody's Knockin'"—Terri Gibbs

"Someone Else's Star"—Bryan White

"Sounds Like Life to Me"—Darryl Worley

"Southern Nights"—Glen Campbell

"Southern Voice"—Tim McGraw

"Stand"—Rascal Flatts

"Stripes"—Brandy Clark

"Take Me Home, Country Roads"—John Denver

"Take Me There"—Rascal Flatts

"Take This Job and Shove It"—Johnny Paycheck

"Ten Thousand Angels"—Mindy McCready

"Tequila Makes Her Clothes Fall Off"—Joe Nichols

"Texas Tornado"—Tracy Lawrence

"Think of You"—Chris Young (Duet with Cassadee Pope)

"Thinkin' About You"—Trisha Yearwood

"This Is Country Music"—Brad Paisley

"Through the Years"—Kenny Rogers

"Ticks"—Brad Paisley

"Tight Fittin' Jeans"—Conway Twitty

"To All the Girls I've Loved Before"—Willie Nelson (with
     Julio Iglesias)

"Toes"—Zac Brown Band

"Trailer Hitch"—Kristian Bush

"T-R-O-U-B-L-E"—Travis Tritt

"TRUE"—George Strait

"The Truth about Men"—Tracy Byrd

"Turn It On"—Eli Young Band

"21 Summer"—Brothers Osborne

"Two Silver Hearts"—Shake Russell

"Voices"—Chris Young

"Walk a Little Straighter"—Billy Currington

"Way Out Here"—Josh Thompson

"We've Got Tonight"—Kenny Rogers & Sheena Easton

"What You Give Away"—Vince Gill

"What's Forever For"—Michael Martin Murphey

"When God-Fearin' Women Get the Blues"
   —Martina McBride
"When I Get Where I'm Going"—Brad Paisley &
   Dolly Parton
"When the Sun Goes Down"—Kenny Chesney
"Whenever You Come Around"—Vince Gill
"Who Are You When I'm Not Looking"—Blake Shelton
"Wish I Didn't Know Now"—Toby Keith
"You Ain't Woman Enough (To Take My Man)"
   —Loretta Lynn
"You and I"—Crystal Gayle and Eddie Rabbitt
"You Decorated My Life"—Kenny Rogers
"You Had Me from Hello"—Kenny Chesney
"You Look So Good in Love"—George Strait
"You Shouldn't Kiss Me Like This"—Toby Keith
"You're Easy on the Eyes"—Terri Clark
"Yours"—Russell Dickerson
"You've Got to Stand for Something"—Aaron Tippin

Please visit this book's website, www.AwfulBeautiful
LifeTheBook.com, for my entire playlist.

A HEART OF TEXAS THANK-YOU TO THE HEART OF NASHVILLE

To the songwriters who touched my heart:

At the beginning of each chapter and throughout my story, I have shared with you the songs that comforted my heart and guided my steps. I included the artists who sing each one because it is often the singer who gives us our first touchpoint with a new song. However, it is the words they sing that sink deep and touch our souls.

I would like to take this opportunity to not only thank but to introduce you to the writers behind these amazing songs. With special thanks to Darryl Worley: Your words so summed up my journey that they became the title of this book. Your willingness to support *Awful Beautiful Life* speaks so clearly of the heart and compassion in the country music industry.

I would also like to thank Frank Liddell for his immeasurable help in navigating Nashville and introducing me to many of these amazing artists and songwriters. I truly do not have the words to express my gratitude for your support and encouragement. I will forever be thankful for your help in sharing my story.

Blessings, Becky

"Awful Beautiful Life"—Harley Allen, Darryl Worley

"Broken Halos"—Mike Henderson, Christopher Alvin Stapleton

"All I Ask for Anymore"—Casey Beathard, Tim James

"Watching You"—Brian White, Rodney Adkins, Steve Dean

"Tequila Makes Her Clothes Fall Off"—Garry Hannan, John Wayne Wiggins

"Wish I Didn't Know Now"—Toby Keith

"If You're Going Through Hell"—Annie Tate, Dave Berg, Sam Tate

"Stripes"—Brandy Lynn Clark, Shane McAnally, Matthew Jenkins

"I Saw God Today"—Rodney Clawson, Monty Criswell, Wade Kirby

"Love Without End"—Aaron Barker

"This Is Country Music"—Brad Paisley, Chris Dubois

"Sounds Like Life"—Phil O'Donnell, Wynn Varble, Darryl Worley

"Thank God I Got Her"—Mia Fieldes, Jonny Diaz

"Trailer Hitch"—Brandon Bush, Kristian Bush, Tim Owens

"Stand"–Blair Daly, Dan Earnest Orton

"Jesus Take the Wheel"—Brett James, Hillary Lindsey, Gordie Sampson

"You've Got to Stand for Something"—Aaron Tippin, William Brock, William Calhoun Jr.

"Me and God"—Josh Turner

"Pray for You"—Jaron Lowenstein, Joel Brentlinger

"Riser"—Steven Thomas Moakler, Travis Meadows

"What You Give Away"—Alan Gordon Anderson, Vince Gill

"Fight Like a Girl"—Kalie Shorr, Hailey Steele, Lena Stone

"Every Storm Runs Out of Rain"—Hillary Lindsey, Gary Allan, Matt Warren

"I Believe in Santa Claus"—Dolly Parton

ACKNOWLEDGMENTS

Katherine, there truly are no words to express how much I have loved working on this book with you. You are an amazing writer, and I wish you were writing this so it sounded better. But I know you know my heart and what I am trying to say. No doubt God brought us together.

Thank you, Keren Baltzer. Thank you for getting "it"! Your vision from the beginning was clearer than mine. Claudia Cross, thank you for helping us navigate this crazy process. Hachette, it has been wonderful working with your amazing team. Karen Sachar, thanks for making taking pictures fun!

Thank you to my attorneys: Monte James, Bill Jones, and Johnny Sutton, aka my Three Wise Men. You are like brothers to me, and I will always be grateful for all you have done for my family. Jerry Frank Jones, Frank Bryan, Al Golden, Frank Ikard, Chuck Meadows, Chuck Grigson, thank you!

Thanks to Suzanne Bell and Katherine James for insisting that Katherine Reay and I talk!

I would have to add a hundred pages to this book to properly thank each person specifically. I wanted to list each creditor by name so you know it is truly an individual and personal thank-you, but at the advice of several creditors, it is a collective thank-you, but nonetheless sincere.

Please take this as a heartfelt thank you and appreciation to all of you, to those listed and those I may have accidentally forgotten—I will kick myself for forgetting later. I hope you all realize what you have meant to me. I could not have made it through this tragedy without you. You were always there for us. I pray you have many blessings in return. You have all loved me and my children well—as God calls us to love: Jill and Mark Adams, Mary Katherine and Pedro Alonso, Susan and Geoff Armstrong, Rona and David Baizer, Dinah and Barry Barksdale, Julie and Mike Baselice, Suzanne and Jim Bell, Jeri and Vaughn Brock, Polly and Brian Crowell, Sherry and David Dalgleish, Kathy and Stuart Dupuy, Diane and Howard Falkenberg, Christie and David Gonzales, Natalie Green, JulieAnn and Doug Hartman, Dealey and David Herndon, Erika and Bryan Herndon, Roe Sharon Hughes, Sharon and David Jamail, Linda and Michael McCaul, Kate and Cary McNair, Tawnya and Jay Quiet, Chrissy and Corey Ray, Teresa and Brett Rodgers, Kathy and Rick Smith, Leslie and Tim Timmerman, Tiffany and Don Willett (bottomless love), Krista and David Wise, Val Armstrong, Joe Beck, Dawn Black, Carlye Carlock, William Cromwell, Ellen Elliott, Virginia Ellis, Betsy Giles, Lolly Harrison, Jocelyn Johnson, Johnita Jones, Brenda Jones, Ginny Jones, Ron King, Kelley McClure, Bill Moretti, Terri

Morrison, Catherine Parks, Mary Pitts, Sally Robb, Monique Riley, Cecily Rodman, Shana Slaughter, Sarah Schwab, Rita Spears, Barrie Spencer, Karen Taylor, Pat Tate, Catherine Wenske, Tracy Wehmeyer, Maria Huerta, Dick Youngscap, Eddie Safady—my favorite banker, Brad Hardin and Tait Moring—my yard guys, Coby and Cody Cotton (Dude Perfect), and Patti Stone and Vera Bowen for their hankies. Patrick Watkins for hiring me at Watkins Insurance Group and allowing me to also work on this book. Every one of the creditors and their attorneys. Judge Herman and Judge Prashner. Matt Gravelle, ASUA Alan Buie, Rhonda Blair from the SEC, FBI agent Holly Kelley, and Don Carnes—John Luke's ad litem. I am truly grateful for your grace and compassion for me and my children. Jim Crane, Julie and Ben Crenshaw, Albert Huddleston, Admiral Bobby Inman, Congressman Michael McCaul, Tim McClure, and Governor Rick Perry for endorsing *Awful Beautiful Life*. And thanks to country music!

To my family: I know this goes without saying, but you are my favorite "F" word: Madison, Boone, John Luke, Mauricio Pallas, my mom and dad (Ellen and Alfred Lee), Hunny and Boomer (Peggy and Boone Powell), Mary Beth, Johnny, Little Johnny, Christopher, Joey, and Allie Arcidiacono, Johnny and Trey Lee, Ryan, Lisa, and Jeff Stedman, Melissa and Ben Howell, Crystal and Grace Colombo, Cari, Russ, Cooper, Cassie, and Catie Kelemen.

Blessings, Becky

Thank you, Becky, for trusting me with your story. I am so honored to have worked on this with you and more honored to call you my friend. You are an inspiration, and I trust I have years to learn and laugh with you. Thank you, Suzanne, for bringing this to me and knowing just the right time to do so. I'll be forever grateful for your patient heart and encouraging spirit.

Thank you, Claudia Cross—agent extraordinaire—for believing in us, and Keren Baltzer—editor extraordinaire—who "got it" at word one. Thank you to all the folks at Hachette, with a special shout-out to Jeana Ledbetter, Patsy Jones, Rudy Kish, Katie Broaddus, and Katie Norris—you've made every step of this journey better than we could have imagined.

Thank you to all Becky's friends and lawyers who trusted me with their memories, as I asked the same questions again and again. You all deserve awards in patience! And to Becky's beautiful children, Madison, Boone, and John Luke...thank you for trusting me with your mom.

As always, I am indebted to my family. Team Reay met the challenge again—tight deadlines, late dinners, lost lists, and missed appointments—and never a word of complaint, but rather constant helping hands. You all are the best and I love you!

Joyfully, Katherine

ABOUT THE AUTHORS

Becky Powell is an insurance agent. She and her three children live in Austin, Texas. Her two elder children, Madison and Boone, have graduated from Baylor University, and her youngest, John Luke, is currently in college. Alongside her career, Becky remains active in her church and volunteer work, including the Helping Hand Home and Young Life.

Katherine Reay is the national best-selling and award-winning author of several novels. She graduated from Northwestern University with a BA and honors in history, and is a member of Phi Beta Kappa. She also holds a master's degree from Northwestern University's Medill School of Journalism. Further publishing credits include *Redbook*, *USA Today*, *Christianity Today*, and *FamilyFiction*. Katherine lives outside Chicago.

Please visit AwfulBeautifulLifeTheBook.com to learn more about Becky, Katherine, and this story.